Anonymous

The Ancient Ones of the Earth

Being the History of the Primitive Alphabet

Anonymous

The Ancient Ones of the Earth
Being the History of the Primitive Alphabet

ISBN/EAN: 9783337088309

Printed in Europe, USA, Canada, Australia, Japan

Cover: Foto ©Thomas Meinert / pixelio.de

More available books at **www.hansebooks.com**

"PALMAM QUI MERUIT FERAT."

קדמי הארץ

OR THE

ANCIENT ONES OF THE EARTH.

BEING THE

History of the Primitive Alphabet,

LATELY DISCOVERED BY THE AUTHOR,

MELBOURNE:
T. HARWOOD, 23 COLLINS STREET EAST.
1864.

THE FRONTISPIECE.

The Symbolical Representation of the Triune Deity dwelling in Light unapproachable, Father, Son, and Spirit, the Glorious Three in One, all merging and becoming absorbed in the Profundity of the Incomprehensible, Eternal, Essence existing, the Great "I AM," dwelling in that state which knows neither beginning, nor end, surrounded by the Radii of his Ineffable Glory.

"And above the firmament that was over their heads was the likeness of a throne, as the appearance of a *Sapphire Stone*."—Ezekiel i. 26.

"And I saw as the colour of *Amber*, as the appearance of fire round about;" "and it had brightness round about."—Ezekiel i. 27.

"This was the appearance of the likeness of the *Glory of the Lord*."—Ezekiel i. 28.

THE MOTTO BETWEEN THE RADII.

"And behold the Glory of the God of Israel came by way of the East."

DEDICATED

To the Subscribers of this Book,

TO MANY OF WHOM *

I AM DEEPLY INDEBTED FOR THE

PROOFS OF

SYMPATHY, KINDNESS AND GENEROUS PATRONAGE,

SHEWN TOWARDS ME

DURING THE PREPARATION OF THIS WORK

FOR THE PRESS.

IN GRATEFUL ACKNOWLEDGMENT.

THE AUTHOR.

LIST OF SUBSCRIBERS.

*Sir Henry Barkly, K.C.B.
Sir Charles Darling, K.C.B.
Sir Redmond Barry
Sir William Stawell
*His Lordship the Catholic Bishop
The Very Reverend Dean Macartney
Anderson, J. B., Malop Street, Geelong
Allan, J. W., South Yarra
*Budd, A. H., Inspector General of Schools
Bleasdale, Rev. Dr., Catholic Cathedral
*Bickford, Rev. J., Sydney
*Broadribb, K. E., St. Kilda
Bunney, B. F., St. Kilda
**Bonwick, J.
Biggs, A. B., Hobart Town
Bromby, Rev. Dr., Grammar School
Buzzard, T. M., Melbourne
Beauchamp, H., Melbourne
Batten, H., Richmond Grammar School
Blair, D., Windsor
Bertram, J., Malop Street, Geelong
*Browning, J., Elizabeth Street
Bindon, J. H., St. Kilda
Bayley T. A., George-street
Binks, W. L., Geelong
Beany, Dr. G.
Ballantyne, Rev. J.
Barnes, R., Union street, Geelong
Carroll, Mrs., Richmond
Connebee, Rev. R., Dunedin

LIST OF SUBSCRIBERS.

	COPIES.
Cairns, Rev. Dr. A., Eastern Hill	1
O'Connor, Murtough	2
M'Caul, Melbourne	1
Crouch, J., St. Kilda	1
Clarke, Rev. J., Sandhurst	1
Christie, J., Crown Lands Office	1
Coates, Mrs., Commercial Road, Prahran	1
Draper, Rev. D. J., St. Kilda	1
Dickson, S. C., Melbourne	1
Dobson, J., St. Kilda	1
Davis, Rev. J. D., Kew	1
Day, Rev. E., Castlemaine	1
Dickenson, C., Windsor	1
Evans, Dr., Richmond	1
Ellery, Robert J., Government Reserve	1
Fulton, Robert, St. Kilda	1
*Fraser, Alexander, St. Kilda	1
Fraser, H., St. Kilda	1
Fraser, A., St. Kilda	1
Fletcher, Rev. W. R., Sandhurst	1
Fulford, John	1
Flint, Wm. S., Invercargill	1
Flint, Ebenezer, Invercargill	1
Fitzgibbon, Edward, Town Hall	1
Fraser, W., Melbourne	1
Fitch, Mr., St. Kilda	1
Fawkner, Hon. J.P., Collingwood	1
Fawkner, W., Oriental Bank	1
Fergusson and Moore, Melbourne	1
*Glaister, Thomas, North Melbourne	1
O'Grady, M., Kew	1
Gilbertson, Rev. J., Kew	1
Gardener, F., St. Kilda	1
*Gosman, Rev. A., St. Kilda	1
Grant, Hon. J. M., Brighton	1
Griffiths, C., St. Kilda	1
**Heales, Hon. R., St. Kilda	1
*Higinbotham, Hon. F., Brighton	1
*Hearn, Professor, University	1

LIST OF SUBSCRIBERS.

ix.

	COPIES.
Hart, W. H., St. Kilda	1
Howitt, G., M.D., Melbourne	1
*Henty, Hon. S. G., Kew	1
*Hervey, Hon. M., St. Kilda	1
Hicks, J., Prahran	1
Hamilton, Rev. Robt., Fitzroy	1
*Henty, J., Kew	1
Hendy, John	1
*Irving, Professor, University	1
Johnston, J. S., St. Kilda	1
Love, William, Kew	1
Lampriere, Dr., St. Kilda	1
Lee, G. W.	1
Lane, Rev. C., Belfast	1
Levitt, S. J., St. Kilda	1
Michie, Hon. A., St. Kilda	1
Melbourne Public Library	2
Mackey, G., LL.D., Temple Court	1
*McCoy, Professor, University	1
*Moir, Rev. C., St. Kilda	1
Mackie, Rev. G., South Yarra	1
McCulloch, the Hon. J., Chief Secretary, St. Kilda	1
McKeane, Richmond	1
Moss, Rev. W., Prahran	1
Middleton, Rev. W., Windsor	1
Merrick, Mrs., Ladies' College, Richmond	1
*Morrison, Alexander, Scotch College	1
*Mackenzie, John, St. Kilda	1
McMichael, Rev. J. C., Collingwood	1
Neale, Rev. F., Prahran	1
Noel, W. B., Commissioner, Kew	1
Oldham, J., St. Kilda	1
Pohlman, R. W.	1
Parliament Library	1
Poore, Rev. J. L.	1
Paterson, J., Windsor	1
*Peterson, W., St. Kilda	1
Paul, Rev. A., St. Kilda	1
Parkin, J., Oxford-street, Collingwood	1

LIST OF SUBSCRIBERS.

	COPIES.
Rolfe, G., St. Kilda	2
Ramsay, Rev. A. M., Melbourne	1
Ray, Robt.	1
Rintel, Rev. Moses, North Melbourne	1
Smith, J. H., Model Schools	1
*Seddon, Rev. D., St. Kilda	1
O'Shanassy, Hon. J., Hawthorn	1
Supreme Court Library, Melbourne	1
**Smith, Robt., St. Kilda	2
Smith, A. J., St. Kilda	1
Smith, Professor, Sydney University	1
**Sargood, F. T., St. Kilda	1
Symons, Rev. J. C., Carlton Gardens	1
Tankard, J., Melbourne	1
Taylor, Rev. J., Melbourne	1
Towle, Dr., Geelong	1
Venables, H., Warrnambool	1
*Wilson, Professor, University, Melbourne	1
Woolcott, R. R., Richmond	1
*Webb, Prout Thos., Geelong	1
Whitney, J., St. Kilda	1
Wilkie, J., St. Kilda	1
Walker, J. F., Richmond	1
Woolley, M., Melbourne	1
Whitby, A. L., Kew	1
Wilson, E., *Argus* Office	1
Wilson, R., St. Kilda	1

PREFACE.

It is the object of the present work to direct the attention of those who feel interested in the question—" Which was the primitive alphabet of man?"—to a discovery made by the author in the year 1848. Being an earnest student of subjects tending to illustrate or authenticate the Holy Scriptures, he formed an humble unit amongst the many thousands who flocked to the British Museum to gaze upon the exhumed remains of a mighty empire, inscribed with records written in a dumb Semitic character, brought to light by Mr. Layard's excavations. It was then he perceived the striking similarity between some of the early Greek letters and the cuneiform characters as exhibited on the Assyrian marbles. He obtained permission from the museum authorities to copy the inscriptions, with a view to their elucidation, and he then collected an alphabet of the earliest Greek letters, principally from Eolian tablets, and by comparing these with the cuneiform inscriptions he found that all the various groups of characters, when dissected, were resolvable into the nineteen letters exhibited in his first column of alphabets. (*Vide* Plate VII.) Subsequent study and investigation have only tended to confirm this first conviction. As soon as he had formed the alphabet, he copied an inscription, and having some slight knowledge of Greek, tried to make it speak in that language; but he could only make out a few names, such as " Assaraoi,"

"Babiloi," and the name of the god "Bel." Thinking next that it might be Hebrew, he applied himself to get a knowledge of that tongue; but scarcely had he mastered the Hebrew alphabet when adverse circumstances compelled him to give up the study of Hebrew, Greek, and the cuneiform writings, for the sterner work of seeking his daily bread sixteen thousand miles from his native land. Previously to his embarking for Australia in 1850, he submitted the discovery to the Rev. W. B. Hollis, of Islington, who expressed a quite favourable opinion of it, and kindly offered to get it published in one of the quarterlies; but the hurry of departure from England prevented the preparation of the manuscript for publication. He landed in Melbourne in January, 1851, but the confusion of colonial life in those early gold days put a stop to all literary pursuits, and from that time until 1859 the papers remained upon the shelf. About that time, having some leisure on hand, he directed his attention once more to the subject, and not hearing of the publication of anything *certain* by the great European philologists,—no literal or perfect translation of any one record, so as to make it quite incontrovertible, having appeared,—he was induced to seek some means of making known a discovery so important to the literary world. Since the year 1859, he has been using every means in his power, under very many difficulties, to make known the discovery. He advertised several times in the principal paper, stating that he was willing to communicate all the particulars to any person who felt an interest in biblical studies, and who would take the trouble of calling upon him. But the only answers he received were from two Hebrew scholars who wanted employment. He sent copies of the alphabet, with particulars, to various learned societies and gentlemen in London, Dublin, and Paris, but he

PREFACE.   xiii.

received only one answer, from Mr. Layard, who tells him that the only plan is to publish the discovery to the world. Nothing, then, remained for him but to bring it before the public in the present shape; and in the following pages he has, he thinks, clearly exhibited the scheme of the primitive alphabet, which is shown to be extremely simple, feasible, and in strict analogy with all the early alphabets both as to the number and the form of the letters. He has only further to hope that this system, in its application by the philologists of Europe, will be found to be *the long-wanted desideratum* for rightly interpreting the most ancient and interesting records of antiquity.

The author feels that the apparent abstruseness of the subject may have the effect of repelling many readers who take up the book merely to glance through it; but even such readers would find, he hopes, on a little closer examination, that the whole book is quite intelligible to any person of average information. The abstruseness lies rather in the *form* than in the *subject-matter*.

He has only to add, by way of preface, that he ventures to hope that the simple fact of a work of this nature, being published in Melbourne, will have the effect of commending it to the attention of many persons, both in the colony and in the mother country, who take an interest in the creation of a local colonial literature.

THE AUTHOR.

Note.—At the author's request I have read over the MS. of the present work, and have made here and there some revisions in the style; but I have not thought myself at liberty to alter or strike out any of the author's statements or arguments.

DAVID BLAIR.

INTRODUCTION.

It has been truly said that "in books are preserved and hoarded the treasures of wisdom and knowledge which the world has accumulated; and it is chiefly by the aid of these they are handed down from one generation to another."* This observation holds good according to the present idea of a *book;* but in the ages preceding the Christian era the expression would have been "in *rolls* are preserved and hoarded," &c. &c. The earliest of such rolls, we are informed, were composed of goat or sheep skins sewed together. Pliny tells us that the ancients, before parchment rolls came into use, wrote upon the leaves of the palm tree and the inner bark of certain other trees. The Greek word βιβλος and the Latin *liber* both mean the inner rind of a tree or plant. The former word has been changed into βιβλιον, "a book," whilst *liber* has remained unchanged. We also find that tablets of wood and of lead were frequently used; and, going back to a still earlier era, we find records written upon cylinders of baked clay; and then we come to the original method of recording the history of passing events, viz., upon rocks, pillars, and slabs of stone. In the primeval times it was upon *stones* that the "treasures of wisdom and knowledge of the world" were preserved and hoarded. This method continued in use from the days of Noah down to the time

* Dean Trench, "On the Study of Words."

of Moses, and probably for many ages afterward. Barnes, in his comments on Job, xix. 23, says:—"The original word, translated, *printed* (חקק, hakak), means properly *to cut in, to hew, to cut* or *engrave* letters on a tablet of lead or stone." Anciently books were made of materials which allowed of this mode of record. Stone would probably be the first material; then metal, bark, leaves, skins, &c. בספר (bsphr), *in the book·* the word ספר (sapher) is derived from ספר (saphar). In Arabic, the kindred word, means to *scrape* or *scratch*—hence, *to write, engrave, record;* and the idea was originally that of *ensculping*, or *engraving on a stone*. Hence the word comes to denote a book of any materials, or made in any form. The art of writing or engraving was known in the time of Job; but there is no evidence that the art of writing on leaves, bark, or vellum, was yet understood. As books in the form in which they are now were then unknown, and as the records were probably preserved on tablets of stone; and as the entire description pertains to something that was *engraved*, and as this sense was conveyed by the Arabic verb from which word ספר (book) is derived, the word *tablet* or some kindred word will better express the sense of the original than "*book.*" We differ a little from Barnes, as to this last word, *sapher*. We are rather inclined to think that it is derived from ספיר (sapphire), "a precious stone." What could be more precious than the sculptured records in the temples and palaces of the East, engraven upon the most sacred and costly materials imbedded in the walls, and preserved with most religious care? We have a kindred word, in strict analogy with sapphire, in *gem*. The expression, "a perfect gem," is familiarly applied to many things besides precious stones, even to pictures and musical compositions; and in like manner the word *sapher* might have been used to express stones that contained valuable documents engraven upon them, intended to be preserved and handed down to posterity. In after times, the Hebrews would naturally have adopted the term, and it would become commonly used for a book, roll, volume, register, a writer or scribe, &c., and also for learning and literature in general. If this be the case, how vastly important are the numberless inscriptions (or *sepharim*), found amongst the ruined cities of the East; and how deeply interesting must be their *true decipherment!*

It will be remembered what great excitement was caused throughout the learned world, in the years 1848-49, by the partial resuscitation of Nineveh's ancient greatness, by means of Mr. Layard's discoveries, and what rivalry there was among the great Oriental scholars of Europe to find out the *key* or *clue* to the elucidation of the inscriptions thus brought to light. Yet some of the most learned men of the present day assert that all that has been done (*i.e.*, in the way of decipherment), *is unsatisfactory, extremely vague, and even contradictory.* The French Academy, indeed, rejects all that has been done, and treats the so-called translations as merely ingenious conjecture. Still, it is not reasonable to suppose that the records of a nation so intimately connected with the early history of the world, should remain long unknown. It is a generally received opinion that in the early ages of the world all the Oriental nations, from Mount Ararat to the banks of the Nile, and from the Persian Gulf to the Mediterranean Sea, spoke the same language, and used the same alphabetical characters in writing. This opinion is fully borne out by a vast mass of concurrent testimony from ancient and modern writers, but especially by that of the Holy Scriptures themselves; for we read in the 11th chapter of Genesis, that "*the life of the whole earth was of one lip and the same words,*" or of one language and of one speech. It is not unreasonable to suppose that this language was the same as that spoken by the great ancestor, Noah, the tenth in a direct line from Adam. Both Adam and Noah conversed with God himself. Now, Adam lived many years contemporaneously with Lamech, the father of Noah. There cannot be a doubt, therefore, that Noah spoke the same primitive language as Adam. Thus it descended from father to son to Abram; and with this language it was that Abram travelled from Ur of the Chaldees, when he fled from their persecutions (for preaching and teaching the worship of the true God, as Josephus tells us) into Canaan, and from thence into Egypt, where he disputed with the priests and learned men of the country. We are informed by the same author that he taught them arithmetic and the science of astronomy: from this it appears that there could be no difficulty of communication between Abram and the Egyptians; in other words, there must have been an identity of language. The primitive language seems also to have been understood by Melchizedek, king of Salem, and very probably by the kings of Shinar and Ellasar, by Chedorlaomer king of Elam, and Tidal king of Gouim (nations). It must, moreover, have been a kindred tongue with that of the inhabitants of Sodom, for Lot dwelt there, and he must have had daily intercourse with its people. The king of Sodom himself had held a conference with Abraham. Further, we find from the sacred writings that the kings and their people just alluded to were descended from the five sons of Shem, the eldest son of Noah. Profane history informs us that Menes, or Mitzraim, grandson of Noah, established himself and reigned in Egypt twenty-six years after the flood, and ninety-five years before the building of Babel. He doubtless spoke the language he had been taught in his childhood by his father, Ham, the son of Noah, and made it the national tongue. If so, the fact would account for the facility of intercourse between the Patriarchs and the Egyptians, and would prove that the language spoken was the same. Jacob communed freely with Pharaoh. It is certain that the Egyptians *then* spoke the original language, which we shall call Hebrew; and it appears from the names of places and persons, and by many other proofs, that wherever Abraham, Isaac, and Jacob wandered, they found the primitive language (or Hebrew) still existing. Here it should be remarked, that the rendering which our English translators have given of Genesis xlii. 23, is not quite correct. The passage reads thus :—" And they knew not that Joseph *understood* them, for he spake unto them by an *interpreter*." The passage thus rendered would lead any one to infer that a foreign language was spoken; but the word שמע (Shmaea), which our translators have made "*understood*," should have been "heard," and this is the rendering of the LXX. The "interpreter" was the המליץ (EMLITS), the officer of the palace, whose duty it was to introduce individuals to the superior or prime minister. The passage, therefore, should read thus :—" And they knew not that Joseph *heard* them, for the *officer* (melitz) *stood between them.*" The 43rd chap., verses 19–23, show that there was no need of an interpreter. As a further proof, we may point to the fact, that when the Israelites returned to Canaan, notwithstanding their intercourse with the Egyptians for several hundred years, and their sojourning in the wilderness above forty years, they spoke the same language as all the nations in their journeyings,—as the Chaldeans, the Amalekites, and Canaanites, &c., spoke. In all their wanderings, they did not, so far as appears, require an interpreter. When they came to the borders of Canaan, Joshua sent spies to Jericho, and in the long colloquy between them and Rahab, it seems perfectly clear that they understood each other's language. There was clearly no need of an interpreter.

It is one of the objects of the present work to endeavour to prove that the language here referred to was the *primitive* language, or *Hebrew;* that it was spoken all over the East up to a very late historical period; and that there is every probability to show that the alphabetical characters used in the earliest ages of the world were those here exhibited.

It is also sought to be shown that in the Assyrian cuneiform characters are to be found the primitive alphabetical character used by man, that our present Roman alphabet is essentially the same as that which was used by Abraham, by Noah, and not improbably by Adam himself; and that the ASSYRIAN language is the PRIMITIVE TONGUE, the TRUE ORIGINAL HEBREW, and THE SOURCE OF ALL LANGUAGES ANCIENT AND MODERN. The book is nothing more than a plain statement of facts and arguments in support of a new theory, entirely antagonistic to any other theory hitherto propounded. The author's principal aim and motive is to add his mite of knowledge to the common stock, by elucidating the mysterious writings found inscribed upon the walls of Nineveh's palaces. The world, after many experimental trials in this direction, is beginning to be awakened to the fact that something *new* is wanting, at once simple, clear, and self-evident. With this end in view the author has been induced to seek this method of making known a discovery, fraught, as he thinks and believes, with much importance to Letters, to Philosophy, and to Religion. At the same time, it is needful to admit that the author feels that it is not for him to carry his theory, or discovery, out to its full development —neither his time nor circumstances in life will permit of it. A more perfect knowledge of the ancient languages is required than he possesses, and he is too far advanced in life to recommence such studies now. But if he can point out the way, if he can give the clue to any whose time and means will enable them to prosecute this work to its full completion, he will feel that he has not lived or laboured wholly in vain.

CONTENTS.

CHAPTER I.

Letters the gift of God—Hebrew the original language—Contradictions of Sir H. Rawlinson throwing a doubt upon the sacred Scriptures—Various opinions of ancient authors as to the antiquity of the Alphabet—Fulfilment of the prophecy by Nahum—Cadmus no mythological personage, but a merchant prince of Phœnicia—An ideal picture of the triumphant pageant of Queen Atossa, or Semiramis the second—The author's application of the primitive Alphabet—Probable results. ... ... Page 1—11

CHAPTER II.

Confusion of sentiment at Babel—The Western nations peopled from the East—Cadmus copied his Alphabet from the Assyrians—Hebrew the universal language—Samaritan Pentateuch—Hebrew poetry and language—Job, Moses, Cadmus, Homer, David and Solomon—Moses wrote in the cuneiform character—The two tables of stone in the British Museum. ... Page 12—30

CHAPTER III.

Author's opinion of the primitive Alphabet—The cuneiform of the Nimroud Palace the earliest character—Sir H. Rawlinson's opinion of the character and language—Greek manuscripts and system of writing—The Sigean inscription—Change in the form of the letters—The Alphabet. ... Page 31—55

CHAPTER IV.

System of Trichotomies throughout the ancient world—"Michaud's Caillou"—The true meaning of the "Golden Wedge of Ophir"—The symbol of the Chaldeans' god Anu, and worshipped by the Chaldeans at Babylon—The Logos—The Ineffable Name. ... ... Page 56—64

CHAPTER V.

Recapitulation of the four preceding chapters—Author's system more fully described—Antagonistic to all other theories—Sir H. Rawlinson's conjectures—Author's translation of an inscription found upon a brick—A new hypothesis—Sir H. Rawlinson's Nineveh—The author's translation—Mr. Layard's Sargon—The author's translation—Ancient inscriptions in support of the new hypothesis—Remarkable coincidences between guesses and the author's translations. ... ... Page 65—74

CHAPTER VI.

The sun worshipped in Assyria under the form of a bull—Translation of an inscription found on the back of a winged bull—Author's discovery of the Assyrian numerals on the Black Marble Obelisk—Annals of Aalfar, Rawlinson's Temen Bar—Rawlinson's great errors in the Assyrian numerals—Translation of inscriptions on two marble ducks—Singular coincidences between the author's theory and the conjectures of Rawlinson and others—Critical notice of the Rev. C. Forster's theory. ... ... Page 75—84

CHAPTER VII.

Rawlinson's Alphabet—Opinion of it by Dr. Wall—Ideographs a term calculated to mystify—Darkness visible—Rawlinson's theory more fully explained—Discrepancy in the history of his Alphabets—His doubts—Rawlinson's translation of Temen Bar's brick—Coincidences—White is black and Black is white—"Pote's Nineveh"—"Bonormi's Nineveh"—Bunsen's opinion of the system of Dr. Hinckes. ... ... Page 85—94

CHAPTER VIII.

No apology for the contents of this chapter—Author's motive for writing—Brandis on "The Assyrian inscriptions and mode of decipherment"—Rawlinson's "I am Darius"—Author's translation to test the primitive Alphabet—Rawlinson's "This Phraortes," &c.—Author's translation—Queries respecting Rawlinson's Alphabet—Inconsistencies and errors in his translations from the Black Marble Obelisk. ... ... Page 95—106

CHAPTER IX.

Cylinder of Tiglath Pilezer—Fox Talbot's defence of Sir H. Rawlinson—Author's answer—Great inconsistencies in the translation, &c., &c.—Rawlinson's confidence in his own works—Rawlinson's anachronism requiring explanation—Author's translation of Rawlinson's "Invocation to the Assyrian gods"—Author's translation from the winged figure—Conclusion. Page 107—118

THE

ANCIENT ONES OF THE EARTH.

CHAPTER I.

Letters the gift of God—Hebrew the Original Language—Contradictions of Sir H. Rawlinson, throwing a doubt upon the Sacred Scriptures — Various opinions of ancient authors as to the antiquity of the Alphabet —The fulfilment of the Prophecy by Nahum—Cadmus no mythological personage, but a merchant prince of Phœnicia—An ideal picture of the triumphant pageant of Queen Atossa, or Semiramis the Second—The Author's application of the Primitive Alphabet—Probable results.

PERHAPS no subject has been involved in greater obscurity, or has caused a greater diversity of opinion amongst writers of both ancient and modern days, than the origin of the alphabet. Scarcely any two writers agree upon the point. It has been a matter of much controversy whether writing be really a human invention, or whether an art so eminently useful to man is not rather to be attributed to a special Divine revelation. Many writers ascribe the invention of letters to the Phœnicians, but without sufficient evidence. Sanchoniatho, the Phœnician historian, who flourished nearly contemporaneously with Moses and Cadmus, when the Assyrian empire was in the zenith of its power and greatness, ascribes the invention to Taaut, the son of Misor, who is said to be the Menes of the Egyptians, or Mitsraim of the Scriptures. Philo, a learned Jew, who lived about A.D. 40, asserts that the invention must be referred to Abraham. Pliny, who no doubt had consulted

B

that magazine of ancient knowledge, the Alexandrian library, says, "As for letters, I am of opinion that they were known in Assyria time out of mind." There is a tradition amongst the Rabbins that Abraham was instructed in literature and the sciences by Shem, and that Isaac also went to Shem's school. Other writers have attributed a knowledge of letters to Adam, and amongst these may be mentioned Brian Walton, the editor of the famous Polyglot Bible. In his prolegomena to that work, he says that "Seth learned letters from Adam, and that from Seth they descended with the original language to Noah and his posterity, with whom they continued till the confusion at Babel, after which, when new characters in progress of time were invented, with new languages, yet *the old were preserved among those who had the primitive tongue.*" Again—"The truth seems to be that letters were an antediluvian invention preserved among the Assyrians or Chaldeans, who were the immediate descendants of Noah, and inhabited those very regions in the neighbourhood where the ark rested, and where that patriarch afterwards resided. This circumstance affords a strong presumption that the use of letters was known before the flood, and afterwards transmitted to the Assyrians and Chaldeans by Noah their progenitor, or, at least, by the immediate ancestors of his family."

Mitford, in his history of Greece, speaking of the origin of letters, says—"Nothing appears so probable as that it (the alphabet) was derived from the antediluvian world, and was lost everywhere in migration for want of convenient materials for its use, but preserved in Chaldea, and hence communicated to Egypt, and such other countries as required a settled government. We conclude, then, that the heathen writers of Egypt, Greece, and Rome, who have, like the modern Hindoos, attributed the discovery of letters to the gods, have only recorded a tradition that has its source in historical truth: for whilst there is nothing improbable in the invention of hieroglyphic writing, the discovery of arbitrary characters, not to denote words or the form of things, but elementary and compound sounds, seems an invention so astonishing, as to eclipse all others, and to lead every devout mind to exclaim, This must be the finger of God! For the man who believes that our Maker intended to elevate the human species by the use of a volume of revelation, must deem it probable that He had provided early methods of securing the sacred records which were to constitute that volume."

The Pentateuch is generally acknowledged to be the most ancient composition extant; and as that is held to have been written or compiled by Moses, it also presupposes, from the nature of its contents, that there must have been a vast mass of historical matter written, according to the primitive fashion upon stones, from which Moses either directly or indirectly drew his materials. The discoveries of late years, by Layard and others, speak plainly as to this fact. As Nineveh and the Assyrian empire had existed for more than 700 years anterior to the Exodus, it is not reasonable to suppose that a nation so far advanced in the arts and sciences should be ignorant of the art of alphabetical writing; and although we have at present no evidence to prove it, still the time may not be far distant when it will be seen that Moses drew largely from the documents and records ספרים (SPHRIM), preserved by the descendants of Shem in the Assyrian archives. Josephus, speaking of the early history of man, says that "those who then lived *noted down* with great accuracy the births and deaths of illustrious men;" and Whiston adds in a note, "these ancient genealogies were first set down by those who then lived, and from them were transmitted down to posterity; which I suppose to be a true account of that matter; for there is no reason to suppose that men were not taught to read and write soon after they were taught to speak; and perhaps all by the *Messiah himself;* who under the Father, was the Creator and Governor of mankind, and who frequently in those early days, appeared unto them."

The Talmudists are of opinion that the *Aramean* was the primitive language, and that Adam and Eve conversed in that language in Paradise. Thus Mars Ibas, the Armenian historian informs us that "Haicus, the son of Togarmah, the grandson of Japhet, being oppressed by Belus king of Babylon (supposed to be Nimrod, the mighty hunter), went forth with his family of 300 persons exclusive of servants, and proceeded northward to the country round about Ararat, and here he incorporated with his followers a number of individuals whom he found living in the most primitive state without form or order. *These people spoke the original language of Noah.* Here they established themselves and laid the foundation of the Armenian empire. The fifth in descent from Haicus was Aram, up to whose time the nation and people had been called *Haics;* Aram, being on strict terms of friendship with Ninus, the reigning king of Nineveh, who not only permitted his reign, but assisted him in the consolidation of his kingdom and the overthrow of his enemies, the chief of whom was Percham of the race of giants, whom they conquered on the plains of Gortouk in Assyria, and the tyrant was killed upon the field of battle." This is partly confirmed by Diodorus Siculus, who says, "The Assyrian king Ninus, assisted by an Arabian chief Ariœus, conquered and killed the then reigning king of Babylon, and made himself master of his dominions." May not this Ariœus be the same as is mentioned by Mars Ibas, Aricus, the son of Aram? Be that as it may, there is much conflicting testimony respecting the identity of this Aram and Ninus, which it is not necessary for our purpose to enter into here; but one thing seems certain—that it was Aram and his son Arah who gave rise to the term Aramean,—a name that subsequently became synonymous with Syrian and Assyrian,—to the nations extending from the mouths of the Euphrates and Tigris, to the Euxine, the River Halys, and to Palestine. The Greeks called them Assyrians, which is the same as Syrians.

The Scriptures inform us that "The beginning of Nimrod's kingdom was Babel, Erech, Accad, and Calnah, in the land of Shinar," and that "out of that land went forth *Asshur,* and built Nineveh, Rehoboth, and Calah, and Resen, a great city between Nineveh and Calah." But Sir H. Rawlinson tells us differently. He says that the Chaldeans appear to have been a branch of the *Hamitic race of Akkad.* He does not tell us, by the way, who this Akkad was, neither do we find this name among the ancient progenitors of the race in the tenth chapter of Genesis. This race, he adds, inhabited Babylonia from the earliest times, and with it originated the art of writing, the building of cities, and all the arts and sciences, and of astronomy in particular. In another place *(Assyrian History and Chronology)* he states "That which can be established without much chance of error is, that at some period anterior to B.C. 2000, probably B.C. 2500 (*i.e.*, 156 years before the Flood), the primitive population of Babylonia was to a certain extent displaced by Turanian tribes from the neighbouring mountains, these immigrant tribes bringing with them the use of letters, and being otherwise far more civilised than the people whom they superseded." Sir H. Rawlinson, as the reader will observe, here contradicts himself, and throws at the same time a doubt upon the Scripture narrative. The presumption is that the art of writing was equally known to all the Cities of the Plain, and that "out of that land (Babylonia) went forth Asshur," carrying with him the use of letters, which he made known to the inhabitants of the cities he subsequently built.

Again, Sir H. Rawlinson says, "When the Semitic tribes established an empire in Assyria in the thirteenth century B.C., they adopted the Akkadian alphabet." Now, does Sir H. Rawlinson mean to say that the Assyrian empire was not in existence until 200 years subsequent to the time of Moses? The Sacred Writings plainly tell us that Asshur built Nineveh, the capital of Assyria; and in the Hebrew copy the word rendered "Assyria" and "Assyrian" is written אשור (ASHUR, in the LXX. Ασσουρ). This is surely proof sufficient that the Assyrian empire took its name from the founder of its capital city, 900 years earlier. What can be the meaning of the following passage in Isaiah (xxiii. 13)?— "Behold the land of the Chaldeans, this people *was not, till the Assyrian founded it for them* that dwelt in the wilderness: they set up the towers thereof, they raised up the palaces thereof."—unless it be that the Assyrian had the priority of the Chaldeans? The Assyrian Belus, beyond question, founded Babylon about A.M. 1900, or B.C. 2100, nearly 100 years before the birth of Abraham.

Dr. Parsons, in his *Remains of Japhet*, supposes letters to have been known to Adam. The Sabians produce a book which they assert to have been written by Adam, but concerning which we have no certain account, no guide to direct us any more than we have concerning the supposed Books of Enoch, some of which Origen tells us were found in Arabia Felix, in the dominions of the Queen of Saba. The Arabians hold traditionally that they received their original alphabet from Ishmael, their present one being the invention of one Ebn Muklah, about the tenth century of the Christian era. They do not appear to have had any alphabet till a short time before Mahomet. Morrah Ben Morrah is said to have introduced an alphabet which was founded on the Syriac Estrangelo character, and in which the Koran was originally written without points, which were, however, added before the end of the first century after the Hegira. This character is called the *Cufic*. For common purposes a running handwriting, known under the name of *Niskhi*, was introduced by Ebn Moklah, and this is the character still in use. When the Koran was first published, there was not a single person in the whole region of Yemen able to read or write Arabic. Sharestan informs us that before Mahomet there were two sects of people, viz., the people of the Book (*i.e.*, book-learned), who knew letters, the Jews and Christians who inhabited Medina, and the Idiots, who lived in Mecca, and who were ignorant of both reading and writing. Hence, the former called Mahomet the "Illiterate Prophet."

Thus we have seen that writing, and of course its elementary characters, the alphabet, were known at a very early period, many ages prior to the birth of Moses; and though we have no direct evidence of their being antediluvian arts, the arguments are so strong, and so numerous in support of the view taken by Mitford and others, that we are compelled to conclude that writing and the alphabet were, in fact, the immediate gift of God to man,—the primal characters being perfect in form and eminently superior in their beautiful simplicity to any that we have now a knowledge of. These original alphabetical characters it is which we are about to exhibit to the scrutiny of the learned, each character bearing the evident impress of its Divine Author.

There existed, far back in the mists of antiquity, a mighty empire and people, who were far advanced in civilisation, and in the arts and sciences, yet so far removed from all authentic records that even the site of their immense capital (Nineveh) has remained unknown for upwards of twenty-four centuries. Only within the memory of the present generation have its long-hidden treasures been discovered, and exposed to the view of the astonished world. These discoveries of Layard literally fulfil the prophecy uttered by Nahum (iii. 6) more than 600 years B.C. :—" And I will cast abominable filth upon thee, and will make thee vile, and will set thee as a gazing stock." A *grave-yard* covered a large section of Nineveh's ancient greatness, and slabs engraved with a pen of iron, and works of art dug from the ruins of her splendid palaces, are placed in the museums of almost all the civilised nations of the world! Ezekiel speaks of the mighty empire which rose first in the order of time, and which, 4000 years since, formed the basis of kingly rule :—" Behold the Assyrian was a cedar in Lebanon with branches and with a shadowing shroud, and of an high stature; and his top was among the thick boughs, his height was exalted above all the trees of the field, and his boughs were multiplied, and his branches became long, because of the multitude of waters, when he shot forth, and under his shadow dwelt all great nations; thus was he fair in his greatness, the cedars in the garden of God could not hide him, nor any tree in the garden of God was like unto him in his beauty." With such a view of the greatness and glory of this mighty empire, can we conceive it possible that it would be wanting in the very essentials of civilisation, and foundation of every science? Or, that its alphabet would fall short, in power or form, of that of any subsequent nation,—for example, of Greece or Rome, whose alphabets are demonstrably derived from the Assyrian, and whose glorious literature enshrines some of the brightest emanations of the human intellect. Assyria had existed as an empire for more than 700 years, and was in the zenith of its power and greatness, when a mythological personage named Cadmus is said to have introduced letters from Phœnicia into Greece; and we are also informed by Herodotus that this Cadmus and the Phœnicians he brought with him "introduced many improvements among the Greeks, and alphabetical writing too, not known among them before that period," (A.M. 2511, or about the time of the Exodus.) The Ionian Greeks inhabited at that time the parts adjacent to Phœnicia, and they having received from thence the art of alphabetical writing employed it with the alteration of some few characters. They confessed that the art was of Phœnician origin. Now, what does the legend of Cadmus mean? Strip him of all his mythological appendages and he will become a merchant prince of Phœnicia. Some ancient writers call him an Egyptian, but the mythology of his name disproves the statement, for by cutting off the Greek termination, υς, we have the letters CDM, forming a Hebrew root (קדם) meaning "east," or "eastern," "precedency," "priority," or "antiquity;" and pointing evidently to the locality of his supposed invention, or the source of the alphabet,—eastward of Phœnicia—and as also being the first, taking precedency of all others, or in the Hebrew idiom, being (קדמ הארץ, or) "*the ancient one of the earth.*" Is not, indeed, the whole history of the Cadmean alphabet simply a myth or legend, expressive of the fact that the sixteen letters introduced into Greece were received from the "ancient ones of the earth?"

But let it be taken for granted that Cadmus was a mere mortal, endowed with the feelings and passions common to humanity, (but very much in advance of the age he lived in); that living amongst a mercantile community, he had imbibed a taste for trade and travelling, and that in the course of his commercial peregrinations, he had visited the great metropolis of the then known world, had seen it in all its glory and magnificence—had been an eye-witness of the pomp and pageantry of a royal triumph—had seen the stately Queen Atossa, in all the ostentation and pride of oriental splendour, emerge from between the colossal-winged bulls, symbolical of the nation's god, that guarded in silent majesty the entrance of her magnificent palace. On she came surrounded by her court, kings, priests and warriors, clothed in rich and gorgeous robes, edged with gold and silken fringe of most exquisite colours, and beautifully embroidered in all their parts; followed by " captains and rulers, clothed in blue most gorgeously, horsemen riding upon horses, all of them desirable young men, girded with girdles, exceeding in dyed attire upon their heads, all of them princes to look to;" mighty men with shields, valiant men in scarlet, chariots, whose splendour of appearance, and lightning-like motion, made them seem like flaming meteors in the broadways of the city. He had heard the noise of the whip, the rattling of the wheels, the prancing of the horses, and the shouts of the multitude, as they welcomed the appearance of Semiramis the Second, and her father Belochus. In the course of his visits to the city of Nineveh he saw the beautiful simplicity and superiority of the primitive Assyrian alphabet over the rough and misshapen characters of the Phœnicians and Pelasgi; and he could also see with true prophetic eye the power it would give him with the people of his own nation, if he were to introduce amongst that semi-barbarous race more refined manners, and the wonderful art of alphabetical writing. It has been observed above that, in introducing the alphabet into Phœnicia, some *few letters were altered*, and this is readily accounted for by the supposition that the introducer, seeing its adaptability to the wants of his own people for the transmisson of their records from generation to generation, might think of appropriating *all* the honour of an inventor to himself. To this end he altered some letters, and invented new ones, and thus accommodated his new alphabet to some rude characters already in use.

The tablet of alphabets will convince even the most sceptical person that all alphabets, ancient and modern, are derived either directly or indirectly from the Assyrian arrow-headed (or cuneiform) characters. The language deduced by means of the primitive alphabet inscribed on the slabs from the Nimroud Palace, proves to be no other than *Hebrew in its most primitive form*. The author in his application of the Hebrew language to the Assyrian cuneiform writing, has been very much confirmed in his views by the fact that all that has been attempted in the way of translation, has given a clear, definite, and indisputable result. This fact leaves little doubt for believing that when the present discovery shall be followed up, when the zeal of the archæologist, and the philologist shall be awakened to pursue the clue given in these pages to its ultimate issue, when the ability of the great Oriental scholars of Europe shall have been brought to bear on this highly interesting but necessarily occult subject, the result will be its complete and final elucidation as an historical inquiry. Hitherto the Assyrian philologists have been but groping in darkness visible, with just sufficient light to show them these dim and shadowy outlines of ancient histories, that have lain for more than forty centuries in doubt and gloom.

And what may we not expect to result in the way of discovery when the language of this ancient people is fully developed? Who can say what treasures of knowledge may not yet lie buried in Nineveh's ancient ruins, and in the mounds around? What arts and sciences long lost to the world may not be brought to light from the archives of her splendid palaces? What precious records, confirming the historical truth of the Sacred Book, may not be found in the mounds of "Nebbe Yunus" and "Nebbe allah Sheth," the tombs of Jonah and Seth, the prophets of God? There is a tradition existing to this day amongst the Orientals that Seth wrote the history and the wisdom of the ages preceding the deluge on both burnt and unburnt bricks or tablets, so that they might never perish; for if water might destroy the unburnt tablets, the burnt ones would still remain; and if a fire should occur, the baked tablets which had been exposed to heat would only become the more hardened. There is another Eastern tradition, to the effect that Noah left behind him ten volumes or tablets on which were written the revelations and commands of God. These tablets, if they ever existed, are now lost; but who can tell whether they may not yet be found, or some trace of them, amongst the ruins of the buried cities of the East? Who can tell what memorials of the antediluvian world, preserved from the deluge, in the primitive *Great Eastern* by Noah, and handed down in the family of Shem to the first rulers of this ancient empire, may not still be discoverable? Who will venture to say what new light may not be thrown upon the historical enigma of the lost ten tribes of Israel, and what influence this may have on the final restoration of God's ancient people to their fatherland, their kingdom, and to the knowledge of the true Messiah? These speculations may appear to some persons as merely the dreams of enthusiasm; but, after all, we have simply indicated here the course of historical investigation and discovery in our own day. Let all preconceived notions upon the subject be cast aside, and let the reader dispassionately examine the theory now submitted to his attention, and we are persuaded that its simplicity, and self-evident truthfulness will satisfy him of its certainty. He may naturally feel surprised that the theory has hitherto escaped the researches and the learning of the scholars of Europe; but the causes of this will appear in the sequel. In fine, whilst the author is fully aware of the importance of the learning required to cope successfully with the many difficulties inseparable from so abstruse and occult a subject, he feels that it is entirely worthy of the deepest research and attention of all who are interested in the advancement of science, philosophy, and true religion.

CHAPTER II.

LANGUAGE.

Confusion of sentiment at Babel—The Western nations peopled from the East—Cadmus copied his alphabet from the Assyrians—Hebrew the universal language—Samaritan Pentateuch—Hebrew poetry and language—Job, Moses, Cadmus, Homer, David and Solomon—Moses wrote in the Cuneiform character—The two tables of stone in the British Museum.

WE shall not enter into a critical disquisition on the nature of language, or attempt to combat the opinions of those who assert that man was created in a state of absolute barbarism, and afterwards became self-civilised and invented language. We may, however, state in passing that we hold firmly by the Scriptural doctrine that man was created *perfect*, with intelligence vastly superior to that of the savage, and fully gifted with the capacity of holding communication with his species. This is the view of the learned Parkhurst, who, in the preface to his "Hebrew Lexicon," says:—" It appears evident from the Mosaic account of the original formation of man, that language was the immediate gift of God to Adam, or that God either taught our first parents to speak, or which comes to the same thing, inspired them with language; and the language thus communicated to the first man was no other than *that Hebrew in which Moses wrote.*" In Dr. Leland's "Advantage and Necessity of the Christian Revelation," we find this view supported:—" From the account given by Moses of the primeval state of man, it appears that he was not left to acquire ideas in the ordinary way, which would have been too tedious and slow as he was circumstanced; but was at once furnished with the knowledge which was then necessary for him. He was immediately endued with the gift of language, which necessarily supposes that he was furnished with a stock of ideas, a specimen of which he gave, in giving names to the inferior animals which were brought before him for that purpose."

But man fell from his original purity. He "sought out many inventions," and sank morally and intellectually. But he did not lose the faculty of speech. God conversed with Adam and Eve, with Cain and Enoch. Enoch walked with God, and held communion with him. God conversed with Noah, over a period of many years during the building of the ark: "And the Lord said unto Noah, Come thou and all thine house into the ark, for thee have I seen righteous before me in this generation." "And God spake unto Noah, saying, Go forth of the ark, thou and thy wife and thy sons, and thy sons' wives with thee." "And God spake unto Noah, and to his sons with him," when he gave them the token in the heavens, the bow in the cloud. God spake also to Abraham, Isaac, and Jacob; and there can scarcely be a doubt that it was in the same language as that which he addressed to Adam and the patriarchs before the flood.

This brings us to what is generally termed the confusion of language at Babel. By a careful study of the Hebrew original of Genesis, we find that the word שפה (rendered "language") will undergo considerable modification. Many critics hold that it does not mean *language* but *confession*. Vitringa states and defends this opinion in the first volume of his "Observationes Sacræ;" and in the course of his disquisition he shows that Hebrew was the language then spoken, and continued to be the universal language long after the event at Babel (noticed in the Introduction). The universal language, therefore, in use before that event does not appear to have been *afterwards* confined to any particular family or tribe. *(Vide* Parkhurst's letter in *Gentleman's Magazine*, May, 1797.) The learned John Hutchinson, in his "Philosophical Works" (Vol. 4, page 17), also enters fully into the subject. He contends that the word שפה (SPHE) means literally *lip*, and should be *confession, sentiment, or religious opinion.* His rendering of the passage is as follows:—" Come, let us go down and confound their *confession.* So Jehovah scattered them abroad over the face of all the earth." " I need only say," he adds, " that שפה (SPHE) is the *lip* ; and when used for the *voice,* the *indication of the mind,* it is never once in the Bible used in any other sense than for *confession.* Before the apostacy at Babel, all men had the same confession and the same words, and one common form ; and, notwithstanding the translation of the Bible, the Jews use the word in that sense in their private writings, and where it cannot be in any other sense. This confusion of *sentiment* was in consequence of the apostates wishing to set up an altar to the NAMES שמים (SHMIM), and so produce a new object of worship ; which was opposed by the true believers. The effect I think was, those who had fallen away from the *true confession,* and were beginning to frame another, instead of agreeing upon a new form for them all, disagreed among themselves about wording it, and the manner and degrees of the service. Each principal gained a party, and each followed the dictates of their respective leader. So each party formed themselves into a *sect,* and each *sect* set up a particular form of confession to their object. It follows that it produced a separation, and forced each, except the *strongest* which it is likely Nimrod headed, to seek a *separate settlement* and so caused a dispersion. . . . And I think I may assert that there is scarce one eminent miracle performed in early times and recorded by Moses, but the latter prophets, nay even apocryphal books, or at least the New Testament refer to it or recite it. I think I may safely affirm that the pretended miracle of the confusion of tongues at Babel is never recited or referred to."

The miracle at Babel was, in fact, a confusion or dispersion of religious sentiments, the like of which has been seen even in modern times ; for instance, the dispersion of the Albigenses, of the Huguenots of France, of the English Puritans and the Covenanters of Scotland, numbers of whom were driven from their native land, and whose descendants now form a new empire in the far West. Changes of time and place will modify any language, and the simple fact of the dispersion of mankind will sufficiently account for all the alterations which language has since undergone. So we read that,—" Out of that land (Babel) went forth Asshur, and founded the cities of Nineveh, Rehoboth, Calah, and Resen." Out of that land, in historical language, went forth Hycus, the son of Togarmah, the grandson of Japhet. To escape from the tyranny of the Assyrian Belus (or Nimrod), he went to the North with his followers, and established himself in the region of Ararat, and founded the kingdom of Armenia.* About 100 years prior to the confusion at Babel—in A.M. 1662—went forth Mitzraim with his sons and followers, and founded the Egyptian Empire. The early ages of Egypt are so enveloped in the mists of antiquity, that it is almost impossible to tell what to believe respecting them; but all accounts tend to prove its Chaldean or Arabian origin. Thus, Diodorus Siculus states that the Egyptians were a colony of Ethiopians; and Scaliger informs us that the Ethiopians called themselves Chaldeans. The shepherd warriors, called Hyksos, who put an end to the old kingdom of Egypt, B.C. 2200, are now admitted by all historians to have been of Semitic origin. Manetho says that these shepherds were Arabians; other authorities call them Phœnicians—a term extended in antiquity to all the Arabian races. Scaliger also tells us that the most elegant and most beautiful of their sacred and profane books are written in a style resembling the Chaldean or Assyrian, and that Egyptian names of persons and places are for the most part reducible to the Hebrew. A still stronger proof of the origin of the Egyptian language is, that the sacred characters of the

* Till the beginning of the fifth century the Armenians, in their writings, used various foreign alphabets—the Persian, the Greek, and the Syriac—particularly the latter; but as the number of characters in these alphabets were insufficient to express all the sounds in the Armenian language, Misrob invented for the use of his countrymen a particular alphabet written from left to right, and originally consisting of thirty-six characters, to which subsequently two more were added. This alphabet, which was introduced in the year A.D. 406, is that which the Armenians still use."—*Penny Cyclopedia.*

Egyptians were Chaldaic. Now, Elam, the son of Shem and brother of Asshur, is considered to have been the founder of the Persian empire. The country where the descendants of Elam settled was denominated *Elymais*, so late as the beginning of the Christian era; and most of the Persian names, which are to be found in the Grecian histories, may be traced to a Chaldaic, Hebrew, or Phœnician origin. Canaan, again, was the progenitor of the Phœnicians, and that people always asserted that they had formerly dwelt upon the Red Sea, and migrating from thence, stationed themselves on the coast of Syria, their first settlement being named Sidon after Canaan's eldest son. All the states and nations which arose afterwards and spread over the regions of Syria (the land of Canaan) spread outwards from Sidon to the Euphrates on the east, and to the boundary line of Egypt on the south. The Sidonians, who built Tyre, were also called Phœnicians—a term supposed to be derived from the great number of palm trees (φοινικος) which grew in the country. It was also called Palestine (from *Pali* a shepherd, and *Sthan* country). Out of that land also, we read—" Went the sons of Javan, Elishah, Tarshish, Kittim and Dodanim; by these were the isles of the Gentiles divided in their lands,"—the many isles of the Grecian Archipelago, the isles of the Mediterranean Sea, &c. The Greeks believed themselves to be *autochthonous*, or to have sprung from the earth; but there is sufficient historical evidence to show that they sprung from the barbarian *Pelasgi*, who wandered from the shores of the Red Sea and arrived in the Peloponnesus about (B.C.) 1760. The Pelasgian alphabet consisted of only sixteen letters. The Pelasgi were subsequently driven out of Thessaly by Deucalion, king of that country, in (B.C.) 1529, when they passed into Italy and settled in that part called Etruria. The Etruscan alphabet is certainly Pelasgic, and its characters were the first letters introduced into Italy. We may notice here the strong resemblance existing between the Etruscan and Cadmean alphabets. There is every probability that the Pelasgic letters had suffered great deterioration from the time of the dispersion, a period of 750 years having elapsed since they had been taken from the original. One remarkable corroborative fact connected with the Pelasgic alphabet is, that it was written from left to right, whereas the Cadmean was written both ways, as we know from the Boustrophedon inscription. This fact of itself does away with the theory of the Phœnician origin of the Cadmean alphabet. The Romans would never acknowledge the Pelasgic letters as Grecian; they knew none older than the Ionic, as appears from the Farnese inscriptions of Herodes Atticus.

Ionia and Eolia being colonised by refugees driven by the Heraclidæ from Bœotia—where Cadmus first introduced the art of writing—and lying adjacent to each other, they may be called the same country; and we may reasonably conclude that they would both use the same alphabet. I mention this because the Cadmean letters, as shown in the subsequent table, are principally copied from Eolian tablets or columns.

The beginnings of the history of India, like those of Egypt and Greece, are lost in the mists of remote antiquity. We have no records that can be relied on of the original peopling of India; but it seems probable that it was first colonised by the descendants of Joktan, for we read in the 10th chapter of Genesis of the sons of Joktan, "that their dwelling was from Mesha as thou goest unto Sephar, a mount of the east." Dr. Muir says there is in the Rig Veda an expression from which it would appear that the ancient inhabitants of India always retained some recollection of having previously lived in a colder country; and he adds that in one of the Bramanas there is a tradition that the progenitor of the Hindus Manu, descended from the northern mountain *after a deluge*, and in all probability formed the origin of the Arian race, and who brought with them the *sixteen rock-inscription letters*, precisely the same number that Cadmus introduced into Greece. In after ages a a people of Japhetic origin certainly settled in India, and brought with them their own dialect, with which the language of the first inhabitants gradually blended, and ultimately became what we call the Sancrit. It appears from the strong affinity existing between this language and others of the same region (and it has since been

c

conclusively established by Dr. Muir), that those forms of speech have all one common origin, and that Sanscrit, Zend, Greek, and Latin are all sisters, the daughters of one mother, or derivations from, and the surviving representatives of one older language, which now no longer exists. Moreover, the races of men who spoke those several languages all descended from one common stock, and their ancestors at a very remote period lived together in some country (out of Hindostan) speaking one language, but afterwards separated to wander from their primitive abodes at various times and in different directions. The comparisons that have been made between the Semitic roots, reduced to their simplest form, and the roots of the Arian languages, have made it more than probable that the material elements with which they both started are originally the same. "There are many persons" (says Professor Max Muller) "who cannot realise the fact that, at a very remote but a very real period in the history of the world, the ancestors of the Homeric poets and of the poets of the Veda must have lived together as members of one and the same race, as speakers of one and the same language."

Thus we have seen that all countries, north, south, east, and west, had been peopled by tribes wandering from one common centre—the plains of Shinar—carrying with them the alphabet and the art of writing in more or less perfection, according to the period that had elapsed since their first departure from the land of their birth; and thus I conclude that Mitzraim, being the first to emigrate from the land of his fathers, had either been brought up wholly ignorant of letters, or else from the nature of his pursuits in after life had entirely forgotten them; so that his descendants, the Egyptians, were obliged to have recourse to the clumsy expedient of pictures to represent letters, words, and sentences. The Phœnicians appear to be the next in order of time and literature, for in their alphabet we have many traces of the original letters. The Etruscan and Pelasgi, if we may judge from their alphabet, must have left the plains of Shinar with a perfect knowledge of letters; but from their wandering life, for a period of 800 years, many of the characters had suffered great deterioration. Still, there are some points of striking likeness in them to the letters of the primitive alphabet.

Mr. Layard is of opinion that the Assyrian writing (cuneiform) is from left to right; and he says that "the Assyrians possessed a highly refined taste in inventing and ornamenting, which the Greeks adopted, with some improvement, in their most classic monuments" (alluding to the familiar honeysuckle ornament). Is it any wonder that Cadmus copied his alphabet from so refined a people?

Sir H. Rawlinson, while he supports this view of the direction of the writing, draws an inference which, as it seems to me, he cannot support. He says—that "the powers of its elements (the Persepolitan cuneiform) were chiefly borrowed from the Greek alphabet, as no other set of letters known to have been in existence and within reach of Persian observation were written from left to right." In another place, he states—that "with regard to the cuneiform characters it is important to observe, that the Assyrian alphabet, with all its cumbrous array of homophones, its many imperfections, and its most inconvenient laxity, continued from the time when it was first organised, from its Egyptian model up to the period probably of Cyrus the Great, to be the one sole, type of writing employed by all the nations of Western Asia, from Syria to the heart of Persia; and what is still more remarkable, the Assyrian alphabet was thus adopted without reference to the language, or even the class of language to which it was required to be applied. There is therefore no doubt but that the alphabets of Assyria, Armenia, Babylonia, Susiana, and of Elymais are, so far as essentials are concerned, one and the same." And yet this Assyrian alphabet, which must have existed at least 700 years prior to Cadmus' introducing his alphabet into Greece, borrowed its phonetic power from the Greek! How is this to be reconciled?

I shall enter more fully into the character of this alphabet subsequently; but my object at present is to show that the earliest languages, whether called Adamic, Noachian, Assyrian, or Hebrew, were essentially one and the same. Nearly all writers on the subject are agreed that Hebrew was spoken all over Arabia, Egypt, Phœnicia, and Armenia, along the coasts of Africa, amongst the various colonies planted by the Phœnicians to Carthage, and even to the Cassiterides or British Isles.* The Hebrew may thus be traced as a native tongue of the East all round the coasts of the Mediterranean. When Moses lived, it appears to be the only medium of communication throughout the known world, and it seems to have continued so up to a very late period. There is strong presumptive evidence that Hebrew was the language spoken by the Assyrians at the time of the preaching of Jonah, who was commanded by God to preach repentance to the effeminate and luxurious King Sardanapalus, his nobles, and the people of Nineveh. Jonah disobeyed the commands, fled to the first seaport, Joppa, paid his fare, and took ship for Tarshish or Tarsus. We are not informed to what country the shipmaster and mariners belonged, but that they were Heathen strangers, speaking the Hebrew tongue, may be gathered from their language to Jonah. "Then said they unto him, 'Tell us? What is thine occupation? and whence comest thou? What is thy country? and of what people art thou?' And he said unto them, 'I am an Hebrew,'" &c. Joppa, being the only seaport possessed by the Jews, had considerable trade with all parts of the coast of the Mediterranean, especially with Tarsus, then a rising colony, and subsequently the most celebrated city of Cilicia. It was situated on the banks of the Cydnus, and was a free city of Greece and Rome. It was here that Alexander the Great nearly lost his life, through bathing while heated in the waters of the Cydnus. Here also Cleopatra paid her celebrated visit to Mark Antony, in all the pomp of eastern

* A colonial author, Mr. J. J. Thomas, in a recently published work, "Britannia Antiquissima," contends that all languages are derived from the Welsh, and all alphabets from the Bardic or Welsh alphabet, which he pompously calls "the mathematically conceived and divinely-formed Cimmerian," for its angular uniqueness of design and style. (See 5th column of alphabets.) There is but little doubt that the Welsh, as well as the Gaelic, is derived, like the Bardic alphabet, from the primitive Hebrew.

splendour. It was also the native city of the Apostle Paul, and hence he styles himself a free-born Roman. Jonah's flight took place in the reign of Jehoash king of Judea, Hazael king of Syria, and about the time of Sardanapalus king of Assyria—that is, A.M. 3142, or B.C. 862. Up to the period when the ten tribes were carried away captive into Assyria, Hebrew was the language of Samaria. The characters employed by the ten tribes in writing Hebrew were, however, totally different from those now in use among the Jews. The Samaritan letters (as they are called) are closely allied to the Phœnician, and appear originally to have been employed by the whole Jewish nation. The Hebrew letters now in use, called the Chaldee or square character, are evidently derived from the Phœnician and Palmyrene; but with regard to the details of the origin of this character, and the time of its introduction, there are great doubts. It has been asserted that the Jews rejected their own divinely-formed letters, only because the Samaritans used them. If there be any truth in this assertion, it is also very probable that they reversed the order of writing, making it read from right to left.

The first intimation we have of a foreign language being spoken in the east is when Rabshakeh was before Jerusalem. Eliakim, and Shebna, and Joah, as we read, said unto Rabshakeh:—"Speak, I pray thee, to thy servants *in the Aramean*, for we understand it, and talk not with us *in the Jews' language* in the ears of the people that are on the wall." Here we have a proof that Hebrew was the language of the Assyrians at the time this happened, or B.C. 710, which was 150 years after Jonah's mission to Nineveh. Again, when Shalmanezer, the conquering king of Assyria, brought men from various cities of Assyria and placed them in the cities of Samaria, they also brought with them the manners and customs of those cities, and without doubt their system of writing also, which could not be any other than the primitive or cuneiform. We are nowhere told that the expelled Jews had any, or cared for any sacred records (the Pentateuch and other sacred books were kept in Jerusalem), for they were sunk into the lowest state of heathenism:

"They set up groves and images on every high hill and under every green tree, and there they burnt incense in all the high places as did the heathen, and wrought wicked things to provoke the Lord to anger; and they left all the commandments of the Lord their God, and made them molten images, even two calves, and made a grove, and worshipped all the host of heaven, and served Baal." The new colonists from the five cities of Assyria brought with them their own gods, and, by worshipping them, brought upon themselves the anger of God; and Josephus informs us that " A plague seized upon them by which they were destroyed; they learned by an oracle which they consulted that they ought to worship the Almighty God as the method for their deliverance, so they sent ambassadors to the king of Assyria, and desired him to send some of those priests of the Israelites whom he had taken captive; and when he sent them, and the people were by them taught the laws and the holy worship of God, they worshipped him in a respectful manner, and the plague ceased immediately; and indeed they continue to make use of the very same customs to this very day." The date and origin of the Samaritan Pentateuch has been hitherto wrapped in mystery; but I think it may be traced to about this time, for it seems to be the most probable conjecture that when the new colonists had become sufficiently enlightened respecting the laws and religion of the Hebrews, and wished to imitate their neighbours in every respect in letters and religious polity: or, it might be that the priests, having their intellectual and spiritual improvement at heart, procured for them a copy of the Pentateuch from the original, which, there can be no doubt, was written in the primitive character. From this time, also, it was, I think, that the Jews began to change their alphabetical characters, making them approximate more to the Phœnician, from (as before observed) a spirit of opposition to the Samaritans.

But to return. We have here a strong confirmation of the identity of the Hebrew language and of its being spoken by the colonists from the five cities of Assyria. The Samaritan Pentateuch being pure Hebrew nearly word for word but written in the

Samaritan character, so that any Hebrew scholar having a knowledge of that character is able to read that ancient document.

Bishop Lowth, in his "Lectures on the Sacred Poetry of the Hebrews," states his opinion that "Job was an inhabitant of Idumea, together with his friends, or at least Arabians of the adjacent country, *all originally of the race of Abram.*" The language, he adds, is "pure Hebrew, although the author appears to have been an Idumean; for it is not improbable that all the posterity of Abraham—Israelites, Idumeans, and Arabians, whether of the family of Keturah or Ishmael—spoke for a considerable time one common language." Finally, Gesenius, the greatest of modern philologists, says in his "Grammar"—"As far as we can trace the Hebrew language, Canaan was its home. It was essentially the language of the Canaanitish or Phœnician race by whom Palestine was inhabited before the immigration of Abraham's posterity, and was with them transferred to Egypt and brought back to Canaan."

It has thus been shown that the Hebrew tongue must have been the language by which God at the Creation communicated his will to Adam; that the same language was spoken by Seth, Enoch, Noah and his immediate descendants; that it was spread by them north, south, east and west; and that it continued to be the one prevailing tongue down to the destruction of Nineveh. With all these facts before us, it does seem astonishing that a people so far advanced in the arts and sciences as the Assyrians, and who must have received all the knowledge they possessed from the patriarchs who survived the Flood, should be so little known: a nation the first and greatest of ancient days, which had flourished for a period of 1500 years—a people who must have been well acquainted with the patriarchs of old, and with the Hebrew nation subsequently to the time of Moses—and yet of whom there is not one authentic historical record known to us, excepting an occasional mention of them in the Holy Scriptures.

If we take a retrospective glance at the early literature of the world, we find that the earliest literary composition we have is the sublime poem of Job. Job is supposed to have lived 184 years before Abram, or B.C. 2180. This poem, if it was originally written in the ancient Hebrew, has been handed down to us by means of nineteen alphabetical letters only. The next in order of time are the writings of Moses, called the Pentateuch, which must also have been written and transmitted down to the present age by the aid of the same nineteen letters. About this period Cadmus introduced letters into Greece and the Greeks began to cultivate literature. About 450 years subsequent to Moses, David, the " sweet singer of Israel," gave forth his inspired poems, and those must have been written with the same nineteen letters; and with the same number Solomon has handed down to posterity his invaluable proverbs and lessons of wisdom. About 150 years later Greece gave birth to the fathers of heathen poetry, Homer and Hesiod, whose immortal works required only an alphabet of sixteen letters to immortalise them in the world's literature. With these facts before us, is it to be imagined for an instant that the great and mighty people, the Assyrians, the forerunners of all nations, from whom the elegant Greeks copied and adopted the manners and customs, the arts and sciences, modes of warfare, style of architecture, weapons of war, and even their systems of religion, should be so far behind all others in literature as to require no less than 150 letters in their alphabet, with 500 variants to those letters, to make known their wants or to express their ideas? No! When the veil that has hitherto concealed Assyria's brightness is removed there will be no more doubt, no conjecture on this subject. The truth will shine forth clear as the noonday sun. Egypt must yield the palm to her ancient, refined, and magnificent sister kingdom, Assyria, as being the cradle of the arts and sciences and the preserver of the greatest of all arts and the foundation of every science, THE ART OF ALPHABETICAL WRITING. From the many facts and arguments brought forward to prove the sameness of the language originally spoken all over the East down, at least, to the time of Moses, is it not reasonable to assume that Moses wrote with the character then prevalent, and that God himself wrote upon the tables of stone in a character understood by the people

THE TWO TABLES OF STONE.

for whom they were especially intended, and that *that character* was no other than the primitive or ancient Hebrew, called the cuneiform?

It may not be amiss to introduce here, by way of episode, a mention of the fact that there are at this moment in the British Museum two stones answering in every respect to the description given of the two stones delivered to Moses at Sinai. They are such stones as a man of ordinary strength could take, one under each arm, and carry a considerable distance. They are written upon both sides, in the earliest cuneiform character, with holes drilled in the thickness of the stone in the lower part, evidently for the purpose of fixing them upon a rod of metal, so that both sides could be seen and read. They are slightly convex, beautifully cut, the edges of the letters being well defined and looking fresh as from the chisel; and they have in fact every appearance of being *miraculously preserved*. The sacred record does not state what became of the two tables of the law and the covenant. We read of them in the account of the dedication of the first temple built by Solomon (2 Chron. v. 10), "There was nothing in the ark save the two tables which Moses put therein at Horeb, when the Lord made a covenant with the children of Israel when they came out of Egypt." We think it probable, however, that at the sacking of the temple by Jehoash, king of Samaria, they were transferred with the ark to Samaria (2 Kings, xiv. 14), "And he (Jehoash) took all the gold and silver, and *all the vessels* that were found in the house of the Lord, and returned to Samaria." This is confirmed by Josephus (Book ix. chap. 9, sec. 3): "He took away the *treasures of God*, and carried off all the gold and silver that was in the king's palace." It is not likely that Jehoash would overlook such precious booty as the ark of the covenant, covered with gold, independently of its sacred contents. This hypothesis may help us to solve the seeming difficulty of the holes being drilled in the bottom. Thus, we may suppose that the Samaritans had heard and read in their copy of the Pentateuch of the awful wonders of Sinai at the giving of the law; and when Jehoash made his triumphant entry into Samaria he was no doubt pressed upon by eager thousands, anxious even to get a glimpse of the precious articles, and to read for themselves the laws of God and his covenant with his ancient people, from the original *Sepharim*. To satisfy their natural curiosity, or even from some higher motive, he caused the stones to be set up in the temple or some other public place, so that all might read for themselves. Just as, in the early days of the Reformation, when the Scriptures were first translated from the original, copies of them were exhibited in the churches chained to the desk, but free for all who chose to come and read. If such was the case, we can easily trace the stones into the capital of the Assyrian empire, Nineveh: for, 117 years subsequent to the sacking of Jerusalem by Jehoash, Shalmanezer, the great king of Assyria, invaded Samaria, and after a siege of three years conquered and sacked the capital, and carried away everything of value into Assyria. The Jewish population he distributed into the various cities of his empire; but the riches and precious part of the booty he carried with him to Nineveh. Now, in the "Journal of the Royal Asiatic Society" (Vol. 15, page 305) are these remarkable words:—"Beneath these eminences (alluding to the mounds of Nimroud), there yet exist *two archaic treasures*, which, if excavations are continued, *must be discovered.*" Let us look at the position in which these two stones were found, and endeavour to form some reasonable conjecture for their being placed in such an extraordinary situation. They were discovered behind one of the human-headed lions* which formed the entrance to the chamber D

---

* The lion appears to be a type of the reigning monarchs of Assyria. Similarly, the Scriptures speak of the lion of the tribe of Judah; and "Judah is a lion's whelp; from the prey, my son, thou art gone up: he stooped down, he couched as a lion, as an old lion; who shall rouse him up." And the prophet, Nahum, proclaiming God's severity against his enemies, the inhabitants of Nineveh, says:—"Where is the dwelling of the lions (the monarchs), and the feeding place of the young lions (his children)? The lion did tear in pieces enough for his whelps, and strangled for his lionesses (wives and concubines), and filled his holes with prey, and his dens with ravin. Behold, I am against thee, saith the Lord of Hosts, and the sword shall devour thy young lions, and I will cut off thy prey from the earth, and the voice of thy messengers shall no more be heard."

in the south-west palace of Nimroud. Mr. Layard says: "It is difficult to determine the original site of the small tablets: they appear to me to have been *built up inside the walls* above the slabs, or to have been *placed behind the slabs themselves;* and this conjecture was confirmed by subsequent discoveries." Let us assume these two tablets to be the original Sinaitic stones, and it is easy to account for their singular position. Tradition had told the Assyrians of the wonders performed by the leader of the Israelitish army in Egypt, of their passage through the Red Sea, and of the many miracles performed by the God of the Hebrews in their transit through the desert. They knew not the God of Abram, of Isaac, and of Jacob, as "the Lord God, merciful and gracious, long-suffering, and abundant in goodness and truth, keeping mercy for thousands, forgiving iniquity, transgression, and sin, and that will by no means clear the guilty." They had heard of his terrible doings, and their hearts fainted within them. The nations around worshipped gods of wood and stone; and from sculptures found at Nineveh it appears that it had been customary for the Assyrians to carry their gods in procession upon the shoulders of men (Isaiah xlvi. 7). As the ark of the Lord had always been borne upon the shoulders of the Levites in all their wanderings, there can be no wonder if they ascribed all the miracles to the ark or to the objects contained in it, as in fact the Ekronites did:—"And it came to pass as the ark of God came to Ekron, that the Ekronites cried out, saying, They have brought about the ark of the God of Israel to us to slay us and our people." And (1 Samuel iv., 7 and 8) "the Philistines were afraid, for they said, God is come into the camp. And they said, Woe unto us! for there hath not been such a thing heretofore. Woe unto us! Who shall deliver us out of the hands of these mighty Gods? *These are the Gods that smote the Egyptians with all the plagues in the wilderness.*" The Assyrians we may suppose had hitherto looked upon the ark with awe and dread, but when taken at Samaria its glory had departed; the God of Israel had given up his ancient people to their own heart's desire; and when Shalmanezer found nothing in the ark save the two stones containing the laws which denounced his own practices and the customs of his nation, what more reasonable than that in the pride and blasphemy of his heart, he resolved upon placing them where they would be as lost for ever? At present we have no dates, but it may perhaps ere long be found that the palace was either being built, or undergoing some extensive repairs, about the time of the Samaritan conquest, or the king may have caused the slab to be removed for the express purpose of hiding, what he imagined to be the actual God of the Israelites. Fourteen years subsequently to this period we hear the insolent and blasphemous language of Sennacherib before the walls of Jerusalem, with the acts of his predecessor, what he had done to the surrounding nations, fresh in his memory:—" Hath any of the gods of the nations delivered his land out of the hand of the king of Assyria? Where are the gods of Hamath and Arphad? Where are the gods of Sepharvaim? and have they delivered SAMARIA OUT OF MY HAND? Who are they among all the gods of these lands, that have delivered their land out of my hand, that the Lord should deliver Jerusalem out of my hand." He thought, in the ignorance of his heart, that the mighty God of Israel was imbedded in the stone walls of his palace, and guarded by the human-headed lion, the genius of his race! Of course, this is but hypothesis. The author has not had any opportunity of learning what may be the nature of the inscriptions upon these two remarkable stones; for, singularly enough, there is no mention of them in the folio volume of inscriptions published at the expense of the Imperial Government under the superintendence of Sir Henry Rawlinson. There is some allusion to them in the *Asiatic Journal* where it is stated that they contain the "Standard Inscription." But is it likely they would have been buried in the wall if they contained any of the records of the empire? As well might we expect to find a genealogical list of kings built up in the wall of a common drain!

But to set this matter at rest and to test this discovery, the author has sent to England a manuscript copy of the Decalogue written in Hebrew, but in the cuneiform character according to the primitive alphabet, to be compared with the inscription on the two stones found at Nineveh. If they do not agree, however, the author's theory will not necessarily be disproved; for they may be inscriptions of another kind. In any case the experiment will be attended with many difficulties. The gentleman to whom the manuscript is consigned knows nothing of the primitive alphabet; but still the comparison might be worked out, the Decalogue containing all the letters of the Hebrew alphabet. Then, in the new alphabet there is no פ (p). It is indeed probable that when the alphabet was given to man it was as concise as possible, having only one sign for each phonetic power,—the sign for b and p, for example, being the same, as b is but a harder p, and p a softer b. The ancients frequently use one for the other, and the Greeks were often doubtful which letter to use. Again, the פ (or ph) will very likely have to be supplied by ו (vau), equivalent to the ancient Greek Digamma f. The q (or ק) will be wanting, but supplied by k (or כ); and lastly, another formidable obstacle will appear in the comparison, namely, the voluminous nature of the inscription.

If we take it for granted that the Decalogue alone was written upon the stones—which would take up but a very small portion of them—it will be difficult to account for the fact that the originals were written *upon both sides*. I think, however, that it will be found, on a careful examination of the Hebrew copy and from many texts of Scripture, that the two stones contained a *law and commandments*. Thus, Exod. xxiv. 12 :—" And the Lord said unto Moses, Come up unto me into the mount, and be there, and I will give thee tables of stone, and a *law and commandments* which I have written, that thou mayest teach them." These are evidently contained in the twentieth, twenty-first, twenty-second chapters, and continued unto the nineteenth verse of the twenty-third chapter of Exodus. Moses, as we know, broke the first two tables. But turn to the thirty-fourth chapter of Exodus, verse one, and note that there follows an epitome of what was contained in the passage just cited. The close of this epitome (26 v.) is in precisely the same words as the close of the commandments (19 v. 23 ch.) : —" Then the Lord said unto Moses, Write thou (this epitome) these words, for *after the tenor of these words*, I have made a covenant with thee and with Israel." This " law and commandments" would require all the space assigned them—*i.e.*, to be written on both sides of the stones; and in this particular the resemblance would be at once seen between the two stones found at Nineveh and the actual two tables delivered to Moses amidst thunderings and lightnings at Sinai.

CHAPTER III.

Author's Opinion of the Primitive Alphabet—The Cuneiform of the Nimroud Palace the Earliest Character—Sir H. Rawlinson's Opinion of the Character and Language—Greek Manuscripts and System of Writing—The Sigæan Inscription—Change in the Form of the Letters—The Alphabet.

ASSUMING then that letters are the direct gift of God to man, we cannot imagine an alphabet planned by Infinite Wisdom to fall short of the utmost perfection. It must be an alphabet free from all defects and redundancies—at least as perfect as the Greek or Roman. Now, there have not yet been discovered two alphabets essentially different—alphabets isolated and unrelated. The progress of learned investigation leads rather to the conclusion that the most dissimilar alphabets must all be traced to one common source, viz. :—The Assyrian cuneiform, found in the Nimroud Palace by Mr. Layard, who says that " these characters long preceded those of Korsabad and Kouyunjik. This is an important fact, as it proves that the *most simple were the earliest*, and that there was a gradual progression towards the most intricate." It was from one of the slabs from the Nimroud Palace the author formed the alphabet seen in the tablet which follows. Sir H. Rawlinson, after expressing an opinion that all alphabets in the East (cuneiform alphabets) were originally one and the same, goes on to say that " there are peculiarities of form, a limitation of usage, an affection for certain characters incidental to the localities, but unquestionably the alphabets are in the main point identical ; but it must be remembered, that not only is the system of Assyrian writing in the last degree obscure, and the language in which the writing is expressed unintelligible, except through the imperfect key of the Behustan inscriptions and the faint analogies of other Semitic tongues (mark this;) but that even if all the tablets hitherto discovered were as certainly to be understood as the memorials of Greece or Rome, we should still be very far from a connected history of the Assyrian Empire." But what can this mean? How can Sir H. Rawlinson undertake to assert this of a people whose language, according to his own account, is *unintelligible* and in the last degree obscure? The earliest Greek inscriptions we possess show not only many of the forms of the primitive Hebrew alphabet, but also the ancient mode of writing from the left hand to the right. The most ancient of them that has come down to us exhibits both methods, and is contained on a tablet which was disinterred upon the promontory of Sigeum, a headland of the Syrian coast, near the site of ancient Troy. This inscription must have been engraved as early as the time of Solomon, or at least 3000 years ago. The inscription begins on the left hand side of the tablet and proceeds to the right, but the next line begins at the right hand and proceeds to the left; and thus it is carried on, each succeeding line beginning where the preceding one finished—a mode of writing which was shortly after superseded by the present one of writing from left to right. In tracing the Greek characters up to the time of Cadmus, and comparing them with the primitive or cuneiform, it is highly interesting and convincing to see the strong likeness existing between the two, and to notice the change that took place as time advanced. (See Plate I.) Figure 1 represents the name of Agesilaus the Spartan king, in the primitive or ancient Hebrew character. Figure 2, the same name in the early Greek or Cadmean; the dotted lines show the alterations supposed to be made by Cadmus—the Awleph or Alpha having its right point obliqued to the right, and a left leg or support given to it. Figure 3 gives the name of the Spartan king in the character of his own time, 500 years subsequent to the introduction of letters by Cadmus. Now, we find that the Awleph or Alpha has a right leg or support added to it; the Gimel or Gamma has a perpendicular line given, which forms the k; and the Lamed or Lambda is turned upon its two points, and altered from an obtuse to an acute angle.

Several of the ancient alphabets will show that they were formed from recollection or conjecture; and it seems that, a few ages after the Confusion, as that part of the earth became over-peopled, the multitudes, in order to escape from the tyranny and oppression of the great ones of the earth, emigrated in large bodies, and settled for a time at various distances from their native land. There might be some among these emigrants who would retain a knowledge of writing, but the common people would in time so confuse the form of the letters, that they would be scarcely recognisable as the same characters. That this in fact took place is evident, from the form of the Pelasgic or Etruscan letters: some of which are erect, some oblique, some turned to the right, and some to the left, but all alike plainly derived from the primitive alphabet. The descendants of Shem however, retained not only the original principle upon which an alphabet was constructed (the triangle), but its proper application in the formation of an alphabet. They took up their dwelling-place not far from the locality of the supposed miracle of the Confusion of tongues. We have already given it as our opinion that long before, God had taught man an alphabetic system of writing. And though very widely diffused, writing is an art which, when once lost, man never again recovers. No tribe or race of man with which we in modern times have become acquainted, has ever succeeded in regaining the art when lost. There are some philologists who assert that the letters of the ancient alphabets are pictorial representations of the sounds or names of the letters; and in the pages that will immediately follow, we shall endeavour to show that this principle is only true with respect to the primitive alphabet. These theorisers do not go back far enough; they go only to the ancient Hebrew, which is a compound of Samaritan and Phœnician; and sometimes to eke out their theories, they bring in the modern Hebrew. In treating of the primitive alphabet, we shall see that all the letters are composed, with but a single exception, of one, two or three triangles, each with a name significant of its figure.

1. 2. 3. 4.

AWLEPH, ALPHA, or A. The names of the letters commence with the sounds they severally signify, which are also Hebrew names of visible objects. The ancient alphabets in use among the Hebrews and the whole race of Shem appear to have been constructed upon this principle, viz.,—the form of a physical object was made the sign of the sound with which its name commenced. It will be seen as we proceed through the alphabet, that this principle will be clearly traceable in the primitive alphabet in nearly every one of the nineteen letters; while in the present or modern Hebrew there is only one, the Vau, which has any resemblance to the object which its sound is supposed to represent, viz., the nail or hook-pin, ו. The first letter is called Awleph, which signifies the *chief* or *head*, as, the head or chief of a family or tribe; and in this sense may be taken as the head of a family or tribe of letters. It also signifies an ox—not from any resemblance between the letter and the figure of an ox, but from the latter being the *chief* or leading animal of the brute creation in its general utility when alive, and also in its forming the principal article of food to man when dead. Awleph also denotes "*beginning or origin,*"—not only because it is in that position from a natural right of precedence, but from its having been the first articulate sound uttered by Adam, being a mere breathing, composed of אוה (AUE), "a breath, desire, or wish proceeding from the heart or soul," and לוה (LUFH), "to be joined to any one," "to adhere to any one," "to accompany," &c. &c. So that the very name of the first letter is expressive of its meaning. The first breath is to be accompanied and joined with others in communicating and making known our wants to our fellow-men. This is the first letter that Cadmus took the liberty of altering; he retained the original

THE ALPHABET.

figure, but slightly inclined it to the right, and gave it the addition of a left leg (as seen No. 2). We find this form of the letter upon the earliest Greek monuments; and, as corroborative proof of its origin, the Greeks gave it the name of Alpha, which is only a transposition of the letters. About 500 years subsequent to the introduction of letters into Greece by Cadmus, in the reign of Agesilaus the Spartan king, we find the Alpha assuming or approximating to its present figure by the addition of a right leg (No. 3); and finally, imperial Rome gave it a little ornamentation, and launched it forth to the world to be used in its present form (No. 4). From an examination of the first letter (see the Tablet of Alphabets) of the Pelasgic, Bardic, ancient Hebrew, and Samaritan, it will be clearly seen that they are deteriorations or departures from the primitive simple Awleph, which is nothing more than an equilateral triangle with its apex to the right. The Phœnicians began to be a little fanciful, the Palmyrenes a little more so, from whom the modern Hebrews have evidently copied their first letter, Awleph.

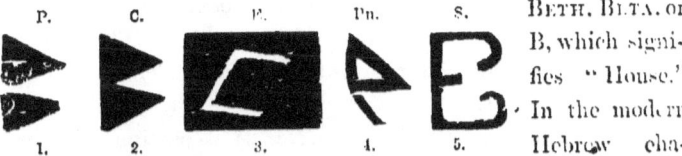

P.   C.   P.   Ph.   S.

1.   2.   3.   4.   5.

BETH, BETA, or B, which signifies "House." In the modern Hebrew character there is not any resemblance to its name; but if we take the Primitive No. 1, and look at it from one point of view, we have the exact representation of the primitive house or tent, with Dawleth the door, and Gesenius, in his Lexicon, says that "its original figure was the Phœnician B (No. 4), and that it more properly represented a tent, as Dawleth did a tent door." It is evident Gesenius never saw the Primitive B, as represented on the Assyrian slabs (No. 1), or he would not have said that the Phœnician was its primitive figure; the fact appears to be, that there was a gradual departure from the original simplicity of the primitive alphabet by the Hamitic tribes, as they wandered from the plains of Shinar. By looking at the Tablet of Alphabets it will be perceived that the

Phœnician and ancient Hebrew are both alike, and there is every probability that the Hebrews, living in close proximity to the Phœnicians, had adopted in some measure the form of their letters. Gradually they merged from the primitive character into the Samaritan, and so continued for ages, until some individual, whose name has not come down to us, blended the Palmyrene and the Phœnician, and gave the Hebrew alphabet its present form. In the Etruscan B (No. 3), we observe a still further departure from the primitive form. There is much obscurity and myth as to the origin of the Etruscans and Pelasgii, but from their alphabet (rude as it is) Asia must claim them as her own; and I take them to be an offshoot of some Hamitic tribe, who wandered from the plains of Shinar to the eastern part of the Red Sea, or northern part of Arabia, at some prehistoric period, and first became known as a wandering people who inhabited a country since called Argolis, about 1700, B.C., until driven out by Deucalion, king of Thessaly, 1529, B.C., when they passed into Italy and settled in that part called Etruria. The Etruscan letters are nearly the same as the Pelasgic, both clearly derived from one common origin, and those were the first letters introduced into Italy; and the Etruscan and Pelasgic alphabet are both characteristic of a wandering, illiterate, and unsettled people.

The Cadmean, or early Greek B (No. 2), is precisely the same in figure as the primitive No. 1, and if we look down the second column of letters in the Tablet of Alphabets which I have named the Cadmean, and which I take to be the one which was introduced by Cadmus into Greece, but whether Cadmus or not, *one thing appears certain*, from the remarkable resemblance between the Cadmean and the primitive, that the one was taken from the Assyrian or primitive, and with some slight alterations (which shall be noticed in their proper places) adopted by the Greeks. In ancient times *b* and *p* were frequently written one for the other, for *p* is only a softer *b*, and *b* a harder *p*. In progress of time, as language and ideas became more refined, they gave the softer sound, half the form of *b*, which forms our present *p*. The *ph* was also supplied by Vau. *f* or *v*, and in the Hebrew language the ב or *b* is frequently sounded as *v*, and as we find from ancient words —from bosco, comes pasco; from labour, comes lapsus; scribo, scripsi; also, sebum, sevum. Therefore, as I have not been able to find in the primitive writing any character, either in form or phonetic power, like our *p*, I conclude that, in the infancy of days, *b* was used for both.

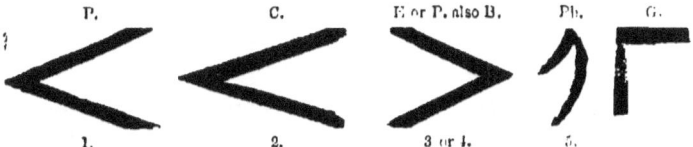

C or Roman G, GIMEL, GAMMA, or G. The name of this letter (according to Gesenius) is to be seen from its Phœnician figure (No. 5), "a rude representation of a camel's neck" (very rude and far-fetched indeed). In our opinion the primitive letter is more probable to be a personification or symbolical representation of גמל (GML), "retribution or return," "to yield or return the fruits," and in this sense applied to the breast of the mother that yields or returns the nourishment she has received to her infant, and who continues to supply it until the child is of sufficient strength to be weaned. Parkhurst says, "when used as a verb active in this sense, it is always applied to the mother or the nurse who suckles the child." If we are to believe that the sounds of the letters represent visible objects, here we have then, the true figure of the breast of a woman, the agent that returns in a life-giving stream the nourishment she had previously received. This idea appears to have been adopted and carried out by the Greeks in the worship given by them to Diana of the Ephesians, as the *magna mater*, or the great mother, who is represented with many breasts, which signified the earth, or Cybele, intimating that the earth gives or returns nourishment to every living creature for the labour bestowed upon her.

גמל, GML, also means "*mature* or *ripe*," and in this sense also the breast of woman is the emblem or symbol of maturity, for, when

38   THE ANCIENT ONES OF THE EARTH.

the breast of the female is fully developed, then is she considered mature, or in a state of puberty. This letter is the forerunner of the Greek Gamma and the Latin c. It will be observed that the primitive (No. 1). Cadmean (No. 2), Etruscan (reversed No. 3), and Bardic (No. 4), are alike; the Roman (No. 5) has degenerated into a semicircle, and the position it holds in the Roman alphabet, answering to that of Gamma in the Greek, is a proof of its derivation from the Gimel of the Hebrew, as also the ancient Hebrew and Samaritan Gimel (*vide* the Tablet of Alphabets) from the Assyrian or primitive. The Greeks, in translating from the Latin, wherever they found the letter c changed it for g or k, for Cajus, writing Γαοις; Cæsar, Καισαρ, &c. &c. The Romans also used c and g indifferently, as Cajus, Cnœus or Gajus, Gnœus, acnom, agnom. And on the pillar of Duilius, erected to commemorate the first naval victory gained by the Romans over the Carthaginians, we read "*Lecio puenandod exfociont*," &c. &c., for "*Legio pugnando effugiunt.*" The ancient Hebrew and the Phœnician Gimel are both alike; the Samaritan is the same as the modern Greek, only turned to the left. All evidently derived from the Assyrian or primitive. This character is also the primitive numeral ten (X.), as seen upon the Black Marble Obelisk and the Bull inscription.

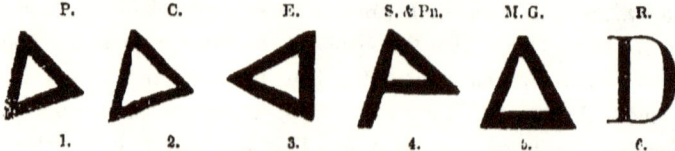

P.   C.   E.   S. & Pn.   M. G.   R.
1.   2.   3.   4.   5.   6.

Daleth, Delta, or D, represents what its name signifies—"A door of a primitive house or tent." In the earliest figures (No. 2) of this letter which are to be seen on Eolian tablets in the British Museum, and in the famous Boustrophedon inscription, the angles of this letter are unequal and come nearer to the primitive (No. 1) than the modern Delta (No. 5). The Etruscan (No. 3), nearly preserves its original figure. The ancient Hebrew, the Phœnician, and the Samaritan are all like the primitive, with the addition of

THE ALPHABET.

a leg, which is found sometimes to the right and sometimes to the
left, according to the direction of the writing. The Latins began
to change the form of this letter about 100 B.C., as we find in the
celebrated Farnese inscriptions by Herodes Atticus, by leaving the
left angle as it was and circumflecting the other two, for the
greater ease in writing. Subsequently they placed it upright, con-
verting the two angles into a semicircle, forming our present D.

HE, EPSILON, or slender E, answering to the ה of the
Hebrews, or Ϛ, Εψιλον of the Greeks. This is one of the
letters of which there is some doubt, and of which all
the Hebrew grammarians fail to give any meaning to its
name. We think it answers to the power and form of slender E or
Επσιλον, and for which, some ages subsequent, the Greeks had the
character Ϛ to distinguish it from their long E or Heta. Ainsworth
tells us that this letter (the 5th) was used both long and short
among the ancient Greeks. It is our opinion that in the primitive
times the Assyrians used both long and short E or He, (ה and
Cheth ח), which is partly corroborated by what Gesenius says
in speaking of Cheth (which is no other than the long E or Heta
of the Greeks):—" While the Hebrew was a living language this
letter had two grades of sound, being uttered feebly in some words
and more strongly in others." This opinion of a duality of sound
as well as of form is greatly strengthened by the close resemblance
existing between the letters He and Cheth in the ancient and
modern Hebrew, Samaritan, and Phœnician (see Tablet). At the
time of the introduction of letters into Greece by Cadmus, only *one*
was used (the 8th), answering to the Cheth of the Hebrew. It is
wanting in the Etruscan and Pelasgic alphabets: the nearest
approach to it in form is the Palmyrene.

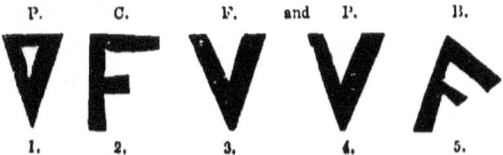

P.	C.	F.	and P.	B.
1.	2.	3.	4.	5.

VAU, DIGAMMA,
F or V. The
primitive Vau
answers to the
modern Hebrew
in form and meaning, viz., nail, peg, or hook; and this is the

only letter in the modern Hebrew alphabet whose form is significant of its name. No. 2 is the Greek Digamma: the Etruscan and Pelasgic (3 and 4) are precisely the same as the primitive, wanting the top outline. The Bardic is the same in shape as the Greek Digamma, and was, no doubt, copied from it: the Greeks turned it first to the right, then to the left. The Eolians used it the latter way, but turned it upside down Ⅎ. Ainsworth tells us the old Latins received this letter from the Eolians, and sometimes turned it into V, instead of OFIS writing OVIS; thereby showing its relationship to the Hebrew Vau, and consequently, to the primitive No. 1. In fact, the Latins made it their twentieth letter V. The Hebrews also gave this character the phonetic power of U; thus we see whence our double U (W) is derived VV. The remaining alphabets have all a strong family likeness. This sixth letter of the primitive and Hebrew alphabets is a most mysterious character. It appears that when "the ancient ones of the earth" had departed from the worship of the true and living God, they retained this character as a threefold symbolical representation of the Deity: 1st., as the element of that God-like gift to man—the alphabet—for through it God spake to man, and man speaks to God in prayer, praise, and meditation; also, as the number 1.—the *first* or the *beginning*—this character forming the primitive numeral I. as seen upon the Black Marble Obelisk, and the Bull inscription from Nineveh. Among the primitive races of men, numbers were considered to have mystic powers, and with this view it was thought the system of notation had some reference to the mythology of the ancients, for in "Rawlinson's Herodotus" we read that "the single wedge, No. 1, was an emblem of the Chaldean's god, Ana or Anu, the head of the *First Triad*." This single character also is the primitive Vau or V, the initial of "*The Word*," in many of the earliest Oriental languages, and the name of the character retained in each language, viz.,—Sanscrit, *Va*-kyam; Tulugu, *Va*-kyamu; Old Canarese, *Va*-keavem; New Canarese, *Va*-kyavu; and Tamul, *Va*-rtic. Lastly, the figure in its horizontal position (as seen upon Michaud's Caillou:—see Vignette on the title-page) is the primitive Lamed, the initial of the *Logos*, the emblem of the Invisible God by whom all things were created. Therefore, I think we may reasonably conclude that the early Chaldeans worshipped darkly under this mysterious form:— 1st. The element of the primitive alphabet. 2ndly. The true figure of the numeral I.—the first, the Alpha, "I am Alpha;" and 3rdly. The symbolical representation of the *Divine Logos*— "Ἐν ἀρχῇ ἦν ὁ Λόγος, καὶ ὁ Λόγος ἦν πρὸς τὸν Θεόν, καὶ Θεὸς ἦν ὁ Λόγος." —"Thy Word is Truth."—"Truth is the personification of the Divine essence." And lastly, in its totality, as their chief god, Ana or Anu. This figure also, in its triple character, is the *Star of the East*, worshipped by the ancient Magi, and proves to be the sacred pentagram, or triple triangle, blending one into the other —the grand arcanum of the Cabalists, discovered according to tradition, to Moses on Mount Sinai, and has been handed down from father to son without interruption, without the use of letters, for they were not permitted to write them down. The study of this pentagram leads all true Magi or wise men to the knowledge of the *Ineffable Name*, which is above every name, and to whom every knee shall bow. Again, in this figure we behold the element or foundation of Freemasonry.

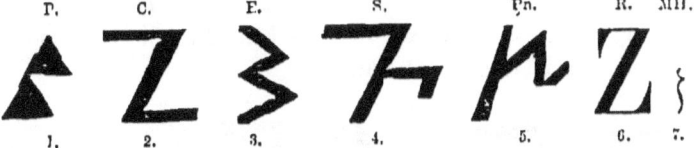

ZAIN, ZETA, or ZED. Some Hebraists contend that the character Zain, ז, is a representation of *a weapon or sword*, amongst whom is Gesenius, who further adds "which this letter resembles in form *in all* the more ancient alphabets." Others again, say it is the picture of armour. Now, with respect to the former likeness, certainly the modern Zain bears a tolerable resemblance to a weapon of some sort, but this will not hold good with any of the more ancient alphabets. The ancient Hebrew character appears to have been lost, unless we allow the Samaritan (No. 4) or the Phœnician

(No. 5) to be the archaic form of the Hebrew letter Zain; in those cases we can see, that they are derived immediately from the primitive (No. 1) as to the signification. I know of *no word* under the letter Zain in all the lexicons I have consulted, that can give any satisfactory meaning; but as the sibilants Zain, Samech, and Sin commute with *Tsade*, under the root זן, znn, (or zanain phonetically), " to be sharp," " to prick," I think we shall yet find its original meaning. Again, as the letter Tsade or Zain interchanges with Gimel, we have גן, gnn, or ganain, " to protect." Now we can see how the primitive letter, with its *sharp, prickly* chevaux-de-frise figure has degenerated into *a weapon of defence, or sword*. Again, as to its original figure resembling *armour*: whether they mean, by the "original," the Samaritan or Phœnician, I am at a loss to know; but this I know for certain, that I have seen in a collection of ancient armour, *a casque and cuirass* very much resembling the primitive character, Zain (No. 1); and this meaning we can trace to the original ganain, " to protect"—*i.e.*, a protection for the body. This point is not of very great consequence, yet so far I think the argument is on our side. The Cadmean (No. 2) is formed from No. 1 by taking away the back and bottom outline and placing the remaining figure upright, which forms our present Z. The Etruscan (No. 3), the Samaritan (No. 4), and Phœnician (No. 5), are all derived from the primitive (No. 1). The Roman (No. 6) is taken from the Cadmean.

P.   C.   E.   Pc.   A. H.   R.
1.   2.   3.   4.   5.   6.

CHETH ח, CH, HETA, H, or E. This letter is the parent of H, and it appears to me that the phonetic power of this primitive character was the long E, but the more modern Greeks were not contented that this letter should retain both the long and short sound, therefore they gave the long sound the form of the ancient Hebrew Cheth (No. 5), which is also the form (with a slight modification) of the

Samaritan, Phœnician, and was copied by the Romans, from whom we have received it in the form of H, all evidently derived from the primitive No. 1. It is, in fact, no other than a hard aspirate invested with the phonetic power of the Hebrew Cheth, and the same as the Greek χ, Chi, *i.e.*, a hard aspirate; and in many Latin words borrowed from the Greek, it is plainly substituted for it, as χάλω, for halo; χάω, for hio; χάμι, humi, &c. And in Latin, michil, nichil for nihi, nihil. Gesenius says that חית Cheth signifies "an enclosure." Where he gets the word I know not. It is not to be found in his "Lexicon," neither is it in "Buxtorf;" but Parkhurst has it with a very different meaning. He says that חית chaith, singular, in regimine, from the root חי "to live" or "life," seems used for the "animal appetite." The nearest approach to in Gesenius is חיל, chail, where he says—" In the Talmudical writers it denotes a space of ten cubits broad round the wall of the temple." In this case, then, it would be something like the figure of the letter (5), " an enclosure." But whether this is the original word from which *chaith* is derived I will not take upon myself to decide. It seems probable.

P.   C.   Po.   E.   B.
1.   2.   3.   4.   5.

YOD, IOTA, or I, יו, which signifies " hand," as the hand of man is the chief organ or instrument of his power and operations. Hence the Hebrew Yod is used in a very extensive manner for power, ability, agency, possession, dominion, and the like. Gesenius says, "that it probably signifies hand, and that it had reference to the Samaritan Yod, a rude representation of three fingers stretched out." We should think it more probable that it had reference to the primitive figure 1. The wedge was used, perhaps, as the symbol of physical and intellectual power: as the wedge is of great importance as a powerful mechanical agent, so the hand appears to be the representative of power, ability, and dominion. In ancient times pillars were erected with the Yod or hand cut or carved upon them to commemorate some particular event, or as a trophy or monument of victory, as can be seen in Gesenius's monuments of Phœnicia: and in various parts of the Old Testament scriptures we find, that it was customary to erect similar structures with the figure of the *hand* cut upon them, emblematical of power and dominion.* And to this day in the East Indies the picture of a hand is the emblem of power and authority. The Yod is also the initial of the Ineffable Name, the source of all power, might, majesty, and dominion. This vowel is often compounded with *e* in the Latin; in Arabic it is also used for *e*, *i*, and *y*, and its initial character is nearly the same as the Hebrew Yod. The Samaritan and the Phœnician Yods are evident wanderings from the original, being the largest in all the ancient alphabets; and this is shown by the allusion to the Yot or Yod, Matthew v. 18: "Verily, I say unto you, till heaven and earth pass one jot or one tittle shall in no wise pass from the law till all be fulfilled." A presumptive proof that the Yod was or had been the smallest letter in the Hebrew alphabet, as it is in the Syriac, Zend (which is the ancient Persian), and the Palmyrene, from which the modern Hebrew is derived. With the above-named exceptions, the form of the primitive letter Yod or I is carried through all the ancient alphabets down to the present Roman. The ancients frequently changed their I into U to strengthen the sound, as for optimus, opt*u*mus, maximus, max*u*mus, &c. The Assyrians also used their Yod or I, as well as their Vau or U, frequently as the same character, as seen on the Black Marble Obelisk, where both are used as the numeral I.

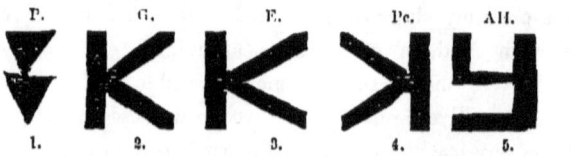

כף, Kaph, Kappa, or Kae, K. Kaph, according to the general acceptation of the word, signifies "a hand bent," or, "the hollow of the hand;" but, whatever the word means,

---

* See Samuel xv. 12. Literally, "*the pillar of the hand.*" 2 Samuel, viii. 3, "*to cut out or carve the hand;*" also, 1 Chronicles xviii. 3.

THE ALPHABET.   45

our lexicon-makers seem to forget that the present Kaph is a modern invention, and that the farther we go back to the primitive age, the less is it like "the hand bent," or "the hollow of the hand." Gesenius says that it also signifies "*anything crooked;*" and this appears to be the right thing in the right place, for if we look at the Tablet of Alphabets we shall find that all the Kaphs are crooked only on one side until we come to the primitive (No. 1); then we see that it is crooked in the fullest sense of the word, for it is crooked on both sides. This primitive letter Kaph, supplies the redundant Koph or Q. It is often commuted for Cheth or Ch, Gimel or C, the third letter. The Latin C answers in phonetic power to K, as Claudius Cæsar, (Klaudios Kaisar).

P.   C.   E. and Pe.   All.   MG.
1.   2.   3 and 4.   5.   6.

R.

L למד, LMD, LAMED, LAMEDA, or L. Ainsworth says that the modern Hebrew character signifies "a goad or spit, which the figure resembles." Ainsworth certainly must have had an obliquity of vision, rendering crooked things straight, and *vice versa*, to say it resembled such an article. If he had said it had the likeness of a reaping-hook, he would have been nearer the mark. Gesenius, a little more modest, says, "It signifies, perhaps, an ox-goad." למד, LMD, signifies "to teach or to train cattle," and with the prefix מ, M, "by," "by reason of,"—*i.e.*, "by means of, teaching." Therefore, it appears very probable, that the Great Teacher of the alphabet to man, knowing in His infinite wisdom, that the letter No. 1 would form the model of the instrument, that would be used by him in after ages for teaching, and training the ox in its duties, for procuring the food necessary for man's existence, gave it the name מלמד, Malamed; or, as the Hebrews have rendered it, "an ox-goad;" or as Aquila renders it, "διδακτερ." "*the teacher;*" and I have now before me an engraving, representing an

Arab driving a yoke of oxen with a sledge, for beating or thrashing out the corn, and in his hand the ox-goad, the very counterpart of the primitive letter, No. 1. This weapon has been used from the earliest ages of the world, and is to be seen in use in Syria at the present day. The Cadmean letter (No. 2), represents the same figure, with a slight departure from its original simplicity, Cadmus having given it a sort of left handle. In the Etruscan and Pelasgic, No. 3 and 4, we see it turned upside down, with the handle elongated. The ancient Hebrew (No. 5), is beginning to assume the Roman shape. The modern Greek, No. 6, is the same as 3 and 4, only its legs are equal, and it is made to stand upon them. No. 7 is the present Roman letter L.

מים, Mem., Mu or Em, seems to be derived from the root ים Im., signifying "tumult or tumultuous motion," hence the sea is called Im, in consequence one would suppose of its liability to be ruffled and raised into tumultuous motion by the action of the wind upon its surface, and hence the wavy character of this letter M. As corroborative proof, the descendants of Mitsraim seem to have had a faint recollection of the principle upon which the primitive alphabet had been constructed, for they have adopted precisely the same figure to represent water. It is possible that the sons of Mitsraim lost the knowledge of an alphabet on their dispersion from the plains of Shinar, and driven to exert their ingenuity, they resorted to the clumsy expedient of hieroglyphical writing to record the facts of their early history. This hypothesis is borne out by a work recently published by M. Frederick Portal, "Les Symboles des Egyptiens compares a ceux des Hebreux," wherein he clearly shows that the significations of the Egyptian signs are nearly the same as the initial, of the corresponding word in Hebrew. A

THE ALPHABET. 47

glance at the Table of Comparative Alphabets will convince the most sceptical that *all* the ancient and modern Ems are derived from this primitive letter No. 1. The Cadmean, No. 2, has been deprived of its top and left side outline.

The Etruscan and Pelasgii being the same people, I look upon No. 4 as the true character, copied from the Cadmean (but reversed). The other (No. 3) seems to be an interpolation. The Samaritan and ancient Hebrew (Nos. 5 and 6) are alike, differing somewhat from the original, still bearing the family likeness. The Bardic and Phœnician (see Table of Alphabets), still bear the primitive characteristics—the three points. The only one that does not show any resemblance to the original is the modern Hebrew נ. Gesenius says, that "the signification of the name is doubtful." He thought so no doubt, from the non-resemblance of the modern character to its name, viz., water. This character also forms the Assyrian numeral three (III.) as seen upon the Black Marble Obelisk.

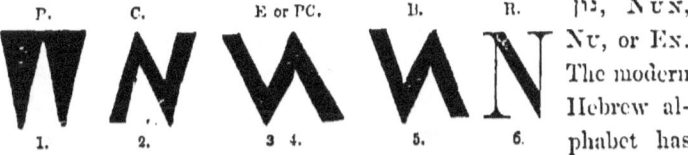

P.   C.   E or PC.   B.   R.   נן, Nun,
                                  Nu, or En.
                                    The modern
                                    Hebrew al-
1.   2.   3 4.   5.   6.   phabet has two forms of this letter—the one used at the beginning and the middle of words, the other at the end; hence the reason (according to some Hebraists) of calling it ן Nun, i.e., "prolonged, drawn out, or perpetuated." Others, again, say it is called Nun, from another signification, i.e., "a child or son," as being the offspring of its mother, Mem. If we take the primitive as the foundation, we shall find there is more truth in the latter signification than the former, as we can see very plainly that *Nun* is taken from Mem, consequently it is the offspring, "child or son," of Mem. Again, it is generally said to signify a fish; but what analogy there is between the modern character and a fish I am at a loss to imagine; but if we take the primitive form of Mem and Nun, we shall see that the latter is taken from the former, or that one is found in the other. i.e., a fish is taken from the water, or a fish is

found in water; or, in plain terms, Nun is taken from Mem, or Nun is found in Mem. But this seems to be too far-fetched to be the right meaning. Gesenius says that the signification "*Fish* does not suit the common square character, but the character in the *original alphabet*, (he cannot mean the primitive) was perhaps still more conformed to its name." This is not the first time that Gesenius alludes darkly to an original alphabet. He seems to think there had been an earlier alphabet than the Samaritan or Phœnician, for he says, in the early part of his "Grammar," that "The Hebrew letters now in use, called the Chaldee or square character, are not of the oldest or original form. On the coins of the Maccabæan princes is found another character, and which, at an earlier period, was probably in general use (alluding to the Samaritan), and which bears a strong resemblance to the Phœnician letter. The Chaldee or square character is also derived from the Phœnician." Subsequently, he says—" The *oldest form* of these letters does not appear even in the Phœnician alphabet." Then, where can we look for this oldest form but in the primitive before us? After all that has been said I am inclined to believe that Nun is from Nin נין, "immediate issue or offspring;" and as the form of the letter is evidently taken from the preceding one, therefore it is its immediate issue or offspring, and in close relationship in form and sound. The Cadmean (No. 2) has its top and left side outline (same as Mem) taken away, and this is precisely the case with Nos. 3, 4, and 5, only the characters are reversed. The Romans (No. 6) placed it upright and gave it a little ornamentation.

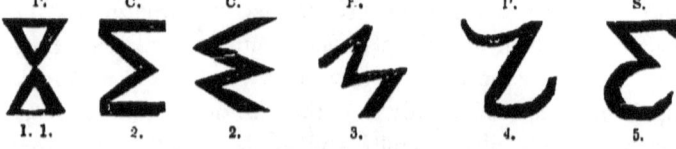

S

11. סמך Samech, Sigma, or Ess. Gesenius appears to be driven to great straits in finding a meaning for the name of this letter. In this instance he says—" Samech is perhaps the same as the Syriac Semka, from its circular figure, a sitting

together, or a bed for support at meals," *i.e.*, according to the Eastern fashion of reclining, as upon a bed, to support them. The Syriac word Semka is evidently derived from the Hebrew Samech, signifying "to sustain, to uphold," or "prop," and by looking at the primitive Samech (No. 1) we see at once the true figure of a prop or support used to this day in all parts of the world, in the various arts of life—rope-dancing, plastering, building—and in that common and primitive *support for the body*, the X bedstead or stretcher. The Greek Sigma (No. 2) is what is called the Scythian bow. Ainsworth says that it is taken from the " Phœnician alphabet without variation." By looking at the Table of Alphabets, we see by the Phœnician character that, instead of the Greek Sigma being taken from it, there is every probability that the Phœnicians had retained somewhat of its original figure, but they could not reconcile it with its name, therefore they added the support or prop to make it like what the name signified. The Assyrians used another form or modification of the Samech, as seen (No. 1,1), and we see the same change of form in the Cadmean (No. 2,2). The alteration that Cadmus made in the primitive was the taking away of the right side outline, leaving the perfect Greek Sigma. The Etruscan (No. 3) is the same figure reversed, but not in its true position. The Samaritan (No. 5) is what we may call a Greco-Romaic, partaking of both forms, but we can see that it is gradually merging into the Roman *s*. This primitive Samech is frequently used upon the Black Marble Obelisk as an initial for Shina, " year."

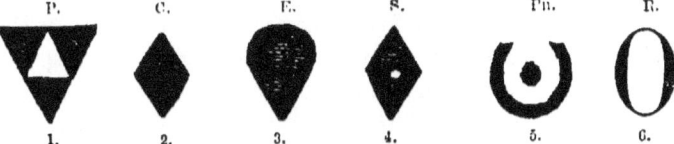

ןיע, OIN, OMICRON, or O, signifying, according to the general rule. " *an eye.*" Where is the resemblance to *an eye* in the modern Hebrew character? Gesenius, to get out of the difficulty, says, " it has reference to the Phœnician Oin (No. 5), which from its round form resembles the human eye." I confess, I am less pleased with the likeness that the primitive character Oin (No. 1) bears to its name than any other letter in the alphabet. Whether the figure No. 1 was meant to represent the long and short *o*, I will not pretend to say; but I think it not at all improbable, for if we are to believe that letters are of Divine origin, we cannot but imagine they were made perfect in every respect for the primitive and future use of man. Although Cadmus at first only took a part of this figure, and gave it the form of little *o*, or Omicron, yet some ages subsequently they (the Greeks) added another letter to their alphabet, and gave it the figure and power of double *o* (ω), Omega, or great *o*. With this view of the subject, the upper portion of the figure No. 1 would form long *o* (ω), and the lower short o (*o*), or Omicron. But leaving this as an open question, and looking at the characters 1 and 2, we shall see that Cadmus deprived No. 1 of its top and upper half right and left outlines, leaving the Diamond (No. 2) a much greater resemblance to the human eye than the Phœnician (No. 5). The Etruscan has the upper part semicircular, approximating to the Roman. The Cadmean (No. 2), the Samaritan (No. 4), and the Bardic (seen in the Tablet) are alike in shape. The Phœnician (No. 5) is growing in likeness to the Roman.

צ Tsadhe, Ts, commuted with Samech, Zain, and Sin. The Hebrew philologists do not appear to have studied very deeply in order to arrive at the signification of this letter. How or when it took the name of *fish hooks* it is impossible to say; perhaps they saw some resemblance in the modern character which induced them to give it that meaning; be that as it may, there is not any word equal in phonetic power that will give it the above signification. Gesenius, at the beginning of the letter Tsadhe, wisely abstains from

THE ALPHABET.   51

saying anything as to the probable meaning of it, for he had previously stated in his "Grammar," that "in many instances the letters exhibit no resemblance to the objects represented by their names." How could they after their modern formation? But let us turn to the primitive, and see what we can make of the letter. In Parkhurst's Lexicon, letter ש Sin, and under the word שדד *Sadad*, we find the meaning "to shatter to pieces, to break all to pieces;" and secondly, "to break or to shatter to pieces the clods of dry ground." And in Gesenius, under the corresponding word *Sadad*, we find it to signify "*to harrow*," and שדה Sade "*a field* or cultivated piece of ground that had undergone the process of harrowing." This last mentioned word appears to be a denominative noun, formed from the primitive noun שד Sad, which can mean nothing else than the *harrow* itself, and the true figure of the primitive letter Tsadhe (No. 1). The Etruscan (No. 3), ancient Hebrew (No. 4), and Samaritan (No. 5) are modifications of the same figure. The Greeks used the letter Z as an equivalent for the Hebrew letter Tsade.

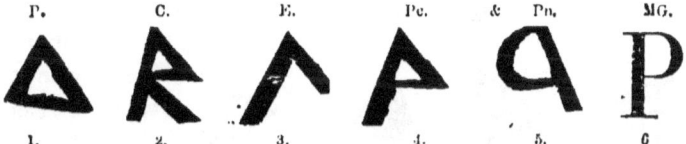

ר, RAESH, RHO, or R. This letter, according to Gesenius, denotes "*the head*," and has reference to the Phœnician (No. 5—reversed), from which, with the head turned back, comes the Greek figure " P, Rho, or R; but the great German scholar forgot that its most archaic form (No. 2) was more like the primitive in shape, subject to the transformation it underwent by the hands of Cadmus. It will be seen (by referring to the Tablet) that the Phœnicians, and some of the early Greeks gave the Rho precisely the same form as the Alpha; also the Phœnician, Samaritan, and ancient Hebrew Dawleth takes the same form; therefore Cadmus displayed his wisdom in adding a right leg (as seen figure No. 2), to distinguish it from the above-named letters. Ainsworth, speaking of the two forms given to this letter by the early Greeks, says: "It seems probable to me that the Latins, observing that the Greeks had two characters for one sound, which they had not in the rest of the alphabet, viz., P and R (Rho), took the former of them into their alphabet for their Pe, judging this figure to be the most significant of the power of half the B, as P is" (see article B). As to its figure, Dr. A. Littleton, Ainsworth, Gesenius, and a host of modern philologists, may strain all their mental and ocular powers to no purpose to make the modern Hebrew letter Raesh significant of its name, "*a head;*" but its primitive form, it seems to me, at once solves the difficulty; for as the first letter in the primitive alphabet (Awleph) is in figure an equilateral triangle, so Raesh also, being in form the same—the symbol of the triune Diety, the great First Cause—the first or highest of its kind in figure, in reference to the primitive Awleph; the Raesh, being obliqued to the right, will be the first change from the original, the *Dawleth* being the second, and *He* the third. By a reference to the Tablet, it will be seen there are four characters in the primitive alphabet which we may call equilateral triangles, but in different positions, for instance—

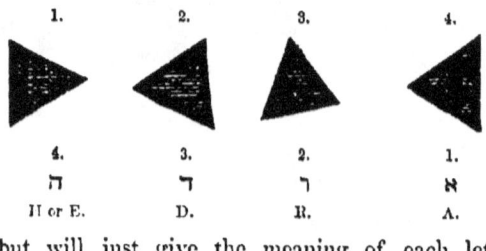

I will not take upon myself to say there is any hidden meaning in the combination of these four characters, but will just give the meaning of each letter in order, and then collectively, and let the reader judge for himself. Awleph, or A (No. 1), signifies either the article "the" or the initial of AL, "*the mighty one;*" Raesh, or R (No. 2), "*the head, first, or beginning;*" Dawleth, or D (No. 3), "a door or entrance;" and HE, H or E (No. 4), though of uncertain meaning, yet it seems to be derived from היה, with a mutable or omissible ה, signifying "*to be*" or "*to exist.*" Therefore, in taking the letters *seriatim* with their meanings, it would seem to read, "The mighty one, the highest or beginning, (is) the door by which we enter into life;" or, taking the last three letters or *one* word (the Trinity in Unity), viz., R D H, it will be "*ruler*," and with the Awleph prefix A, "the ruler" or "mighty ruler:" ergo, "*the mysterious Three in One, the Almighty Ruler.*"

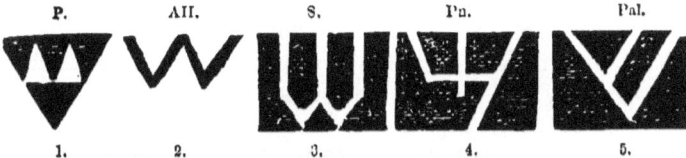

ש, SHIN or SH. We have no double corresponding letters either in the Cadmean, Etruscan, or Pelasgic; but we have a close resemblance to it in the ancient Hebrew (No. 2), and carried through the Samaritan (No. 3), Phœnician (No. 4), and Palmyrene (No. 5), to the modern Hebrew. There are two characters alike in form in the modern Hebrew alphabet—viz., שׁ, Sh, Shin, and שׂ, Sin, distinguished only by the diacritic point. *Sin* differed little or nothing from (ס) Samech in phonetic power; neither is it in accordance with the simplicity of the primitive alphabets to have two letters with one sound. Again, as I have endeavoured to show, every primitive letter has a meaning significant of its form; and there cannot be seen, with all the arbitrary straining possible, the least affinity or likeness between the character ש, Sin, and the meaning its name gives us,—viz., "*mud or mire.*" The Arabians have no Samech, but use Sin instead, and the Syrians use their Semka for both. Gesenius (who is considered the greatest authority in these matters) says, "that *Shin* and *Sin* were originally the same letter, pronounced without doubt as *Sh*, and in unpointed Hebrew this is still the same." In the course of time, when the Hebrew alphabet underwent some considerable change from the ancient Hebrew form to the present modern figure, the Hebrews thought it necessary to adopt Sin into their alphabet, for no other reason it would seem than that the Arabians used it as well as the Syrians. From these premises, it must be evident that *Sin* is a letter redundant, and consequently was not to be found in the primitive alphabet.

Shin ש, signifies tooth or teeth, which, says Gesenius "is derived from the pronged form of the letter in all the Shemitish alphabets," and which can be seen from the five ancient letters at the head of this article (from 2 to 5), all evidently derived from the primitive No. 1, the hieroglyphical representation of five teeth, three upper and two lower, closely locked in each other. This character is also used as the Assyrian or primitive numeral IV. consisting of four elements, as seen upon the Black Marble Obelisk.

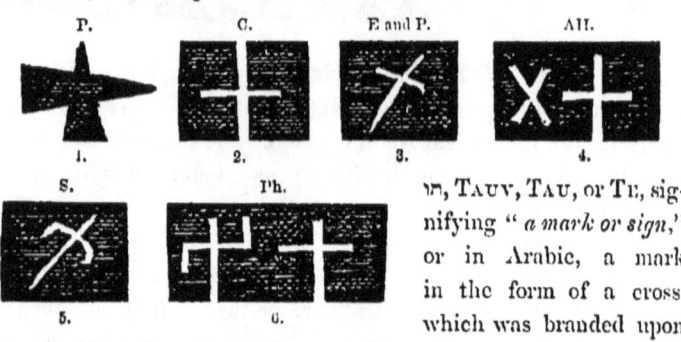

ת, Tauv, Tau, or Te, signifying "*a mark or sign*," or in Arabic, a mark in the form of a cross, which was branded upon the flanks and necks of horses and camels. Hence, probably (says Gesenius), the name of the letter Tauv, or T, which in the ancient Hebrew, Samaritan, and Phœnician, has the form of a cross (see figures 5 and 6), and from which the Greeks and Romans took the form of their T, and as the Latins from the Greeks, so the Greeks from the ancient Hebrew: or, more properly speaking, the early Greek, by means of Cadmus, borrowed the form of their letter T from the fountain-head—the Assyrian or primitive (see figures 1 and 2). The word *Tauv* is also used in a final sense, as "an extremity," "bound or finish." Being the last letter in the Hebrew and early Greek alphabets, it was used as a subscription or final mark to writings or documents; —even to the present day the illiterate who cannot sign their name make their mark or sign the X cross. May not this letter be a type or sign prepared and designed by God to prefigure some future thing or event, or to be, as St. Paul says, "*a shadow of things to come?*" It is generally allowed, and

THE ALPHABET.

proved by the New Testament Scriptures, that the whole of the Mosaic ceremonial law was a typical institution. Is it *too* much to say that many, if not all the letters of the primitive alphabet partake of this typical character? In the Revelation by St. John we have our Lord saying, " I am Alpha and Omega—the beginning and the ending." Again, " I am Alpha and Omega—the first and the last." This was addressed to the Greek church; and in that age, Omega was the last letter in the Greek alphabet. If it had been addressed to the Jewish nation, when Hebrew was the almost universal language, there would have been much more significance in the words, *I am Awleph and Tauv —the first and the last :* the first and last letters of the Hebrew alphabet signifying " *the beginning and finish,*" which latter sense is not conveyed in the Greek Omega, which means nothing more than great O; and as I have endeavoured to show that every primitive letter has a significant or symbolical meaning, may not this letter I say, be typical of the completion of that great and glorious work, the redemption of man, when we find its Divine Author, the Lord of Light and Glory, the mighty God, the mysterious Word, signing the Divine compact between God and man with his own precious blood, upon the Tauv or Cross, and exclaiming with his expiring breath; "*It is finished!*"

CHAPTER IV.

A system of Trichotomies throughout the ancient world—"Michaud's Caillou"—The true meaning of the "Golden Wedge of Ophir"—The symbol of the Chaldeans' god Anu, and worshipped by the Chaldeans at Babylon—The Logos—The Ineffable Name.

FROM the earliest ages there has been in the human mind an idea of a triplicity, or triadism, or (as some call it) a trichotomy, and hence the number three has become a sacred number, and almost every nation retains the idea of a triadism in its religious rites. The origin of this idea is involved in great obscurity, but all writers ascribe to it the greatest antiquity. The most ancient symbol used by the Jews in writing the mysterious Ineffable Name was by three *yods* in a circle (Plate I., fig. 4), but this was relinquished in consequence of Christians having used it in demonstrating the doctrine of the Trinity. The Cabalists use a triangular form of the same great and holy Name, applicable to the Being who *was*, and *is*, and ever *will be*,—the ESSENCE existing (Pl. 1, fig. 6, and also in the form of fig. 5). In the book of Job there is exhibited throughout a regular and all-pervading series of Trichotomies. The Neoplatonists asserted that triadism was a theology given by Divine Revelation. It seems, therefore, to have been adopted by the earliest races of men; in Phœnicia, in their Cronos, Jupiter Belus and Apollo; in India, in Brahma, Vishnu and Seeva. And not only in the systems of religion, but the idea was retained in their temples and tombs. Thus, Herodotus informs us that the temple of Belus at Babylon was pyramidal, and it is well known that pagan nations in all parts of the world used the same form in their sacred buildings; for instance, the pyramids of Egypt, and the tombs of Etruria. Even the architectural remains of Mexico, from their resemblance to the pyramidal structures of the East, give to the antiquary an idea of a common origin with them. The inhabitants of Thebes, Lemnos, Macedonia, but more particularly the islands of Samothracia and Imbros, worshipped a trinity of deities under the name of the Cabiri. It is uncertain where their worship was first established; but it appears from Faber's "Mysteries of the Cabiri," that it took its rise in Babylonia. He says:—"The attempt of Nimrod to force his abominations upon the reluctant consciences of mankind, produced a war between his followers and those who still persevered in commemorating the event of the deluge, and who rejected with horror the profane reveries of Sabeanism;* the ark festival was converted into a superstitious idolatry, and was for ever united with the worship of the heavenly bodies. The mysteries of the Cabiri are, in fact, nothing more than a mythological account of these events; and they will be found throughout to refer at once to the catastrophe of the Deluge, and to the impious rites of that Sabeanism which was united by Nimrod with the arkite superstition." Diodorus Siculus informs us that the Samothracians had a peculiar dialect of their own which prevailed in their sacred rites; and Jamblichus, in his work on the "Mysteries of the Egyptians," tells us plainly that "the language used in the

* The term Sabeanism is derived from the Hebrew word צבא Zaba, "a host," and is employed to express what was probably the earliest form of Polytheism, which consisted in the worship of the sun, moon, and stars,— called the host of heaven. It is probable that the worship of the heavenly bodies originated partly in an indistinct tradition of a primitive revelation, and partly in a kind of rude natural theology of the human mind. It requires no stretch of faith to believe that, on the assumption of a primeval revelation, some broken traditions would be handed down by the antediluvian patriarchs, and by the immediate descendants of Noah, about the rule of the sun by day, and the moon by night, and about the sun being the "greater light," and the moon "a lesser light." The tradition of such a power and influence being given to the sun and moon, when it came to work upon the fervid and corrupt imaginations of Oriental people, would be very likely to incline them to ascribe divinity to those creatures whose majesty appeared so glorious and whose influence was so extensive and benign. Sabeanism, therefore, first arose in Chaldea, was soon introduced into Egypt, and thence carried into Greece.

mysteries of the Cabiri was not that of Greece, but of Egypt and Assyria; that the language of the mysteries was the language of the gods,—the first and most ancient language that was spoken upon earth,—and that this language was the Chaldee or Hebrew." According to Sanchoniatho, the mysteries were adopted by the Phœnicians, from whence they were carried into Greece by the Pelasgi. But perhaps the strongest of all argument will be found in the remarkable stone altar found amongst the ruins of Babylon, and now preserved in the Bibliotheque Nationale at Paris. (See Vignette, title page). From this altar it is seen that this figure had been worshipped in Chaldea as a sacred object, either as the basis or element of the primitive written character, or of some emblematical meaning attached to its form. Mr. Layard seems to have anticipated the employment of this interesting relic, as an argument in favour of some new theory of this kind, for he says in a note—"It would not be difficult for those who are apt at discovering the hidden meaning of ancient symbols to invest the arrowhead or wedge of the Assyrian characters, assuming, as it frequently does, the form of an equilateral triangle, with sacred and mythic properties, and to find in it a direct illustration of the sacred triad, the basis of Chaldean worship and theogony, or of another well-known Eastern object of worship." This anticipation has now been realised; and in proof, let the reader attend to the following rendering of the 12th verse of the 13th chapter of Isaiah, especially the latter part of the verse, where mention is made of " The golden wedge of Ophir." The original word is מכתם (Mikkethem), rendered, "than the golden wedge." Let us analyse and see what it means. מ (M) is a particle prefix, signifying " more than ;" and כתם (KeTHeM) is rendered by some Hebraists " golden," which it cannot be, since there is no form to which the adjective can apply. Parkhurst says it means " to mark with a graver, impression, stamp, or the like." And if we commute the M for B (which is commonly done) we have כתב (KeTHeB), which is a " Song of praise, a poem, a writing," something written, a book, *a word, a letter (literæ elementum).* Hence, the meaning will be,

"More than the letter (or word) of Ophir." The whole verse in the original is—אוקיר אנוש מפז ואדם מכתם אופיר—"I will purify man more than fine gold, even men more that the *letter* (or word) of Ophir." The Hebrew scholar will perceive that there is no word in the passage quoted that could possibly be rendered "wedge." In Joshua (chap. vii. 21-24), where the cupidity of Achan is discovered, the ingot of gold is called LASHON ZEEB, or the "tongue of gold," which our translators have rendered "wedge of gold," from the tongue being of a wedge-like shape. Now, had the passage in Isaiah been LASHON ZEEB AOPHIR, or "the golden tongue of Ophir," it might have been properly rendered, "The golden wedge of Ophir," but it is not so. Michaud's stone was found at Babylon, or in its neighbourhood. Upon the altar is the single wedge, evidently for the purpose of being worshipped. This single wedge is the symbol of the Chaldean god ANI or ANU; and, according to Rawlinson in his "Five Ancient Monarchies," is manifestly invested with a phonetic power corresponding to the name of the god. In this sense it is "the Word," and this word Ani is the name of the God of Israel, revealed to Moses on the mountain of Horeb—the great "I AM." Again, the single wedge is the true figure of the numeral I, as discovered by the author on the Black Marble Obelisk, and as it is well known that numbers, amongst the early Chaldeans, were supposed to be invested with mystic powers, this numeral I. comes into immediate contact with the Chaldean mythology, as being the representative of the god ANI or ANU—the first of the Chaldean sacred triad.*

* I do not adopt the opinions of Rawlinson as my own with respect to the god ANU. I mention them only as singular coincidences, and strong collateral evidences of the truth of my own theory. Whenever the Messrs. Rawlinsons have recourse to the cuneiform they seem to get into a maze, from which they can only escape by attributing all the difficulties to the ignorance, the carelessness, and laxity of the ancients. For instance, they think they have determined the name of the god ANU, as the first of the triad ; but they add, "The phonetic reading of the second god of the triad is a matter of speculation,—BIL NIPRIT,—but through the many inconsistencies in the employment of cuneiform groups for Bil, &c., with or without any adjuncts, which make it most difficult to distinguish between one and the other. From this we infer that the mythological system itself, as well as its mode of expression, was to the last degree lax and fluctuating."

It is evident that the passage quoted above has reference to something very precious in Ophir. The original object worshipped in the days of Isaiah might have been made of the purest gold, (like the golden calf of the Israelites), and worshipped as "The word." Perhaps, moreover, this golden "word" was lost or carried away through the incursion of some neighbouring king, and the people of Ophir, to supply its place, made a similar object in stone that it might not awaken the cupidity of any subsequent conqueror. This opinion is partly confirmed by the rendering of the passage in Isaiah by the LXX :—" Μᾶλλον ἔντιμος ἔσται ἢ ὁ λιθός ὁ ἐν Σουφιρ." "More precious will be than the *stone in Ophir*." This rendering also seems to confirm the idea that the original "word or letter" had reference to the Trinity. Else why not have rendered it according to the original, "The word?" We all know how very careful the Jews were in expunging or mistranslating anything that had reference to the Glorious Three in One. The Babylonians worshipped signs, images, or representations of ideas or powers of their various gods ; and as the things are mentioned we have only to guess at their ideas, as to how those signs were like the things, or powers, or actions they imagined those signs represented. We find they used images, carved, molten, or engraved ; some of them borne on carriages, some by beasts, some by men ; and some small images which were light and portable in a small compass ; and sometimes they made the creatures themselves signs of the things or powers they worshipped. Philostratus, a Grecian philosopher, who lived in the early part of the third century, says :—"There was in the Royal Palace at Babylon, a room vaulted like a heaven, with representations of gods placed aloft, and appearing as it were in the air, that the king was wont to give judgment there ; and that there were four golden wedge-shaped Ινγγες or charms hanging down from the roof, prepared by the magicians or wise men, and called Θεων γλωτται or tongues of the gods, and by means of those tongues of gold the judgments of the king would become Divine oracles, and be so esteemed by their subjects."

THE LOGOS.

The word "tongue" often occurs in the Scriptures to denote language or speech; and the peculiar appearance of cloven tongues on the day of Pentecost, was emblematical of the diversity of languages which the apostles were about to be able to utter. In the monument of antiquity before us, we have the symbol of the Chaldeans' god ANI, or ANU; the true figure of the numeral I., the first, the Alpha, and also the emblem of the *tongue*, the *organ of speech*, or the *word;* and what is more remarkable, it is the Vau in the primitive alphabet, the initial letter of "*The word*" in several of the primitive languages. (See article Vau in the History of the Alphabet, chap. III.) Another singular coincidence is that the figure in its horizontal position is the Lamed or Lambda, the initial of the Divine word the *Logos.* There is an inscription upon this altar which I regret that I have not been able to obtain a copy of; no doubt it would tend to enlighten this mysterious subject.

I shall add here some extracts from various authors on the Divine Logos, and the Ineffable name, which may throw additional light upon this interesting subject:—

"Philo, the Alexandrian Jew, speaks of 'the most holy "Word" [Logos] as the image of the absolutely existing Being, as the first begotten Son, who like the viceroy of a great king was to be charged with the government of the whole creation; as the Man of God immortal and incorruptible; and as the agent in the creation of the world.' Philo used many more expressions with regard to the 'Word,' often dark and mystical, and mingled with notions borrowed from the Platonic philosophy, but yet such as we cannot read without something even of wonder. Thus: 'The Divine Word discerns most acutely, who is sufficient to see into all things, by whom we may see whatever is worth seeing. What is more refulgent or more radiant than the Word of God?' 'The Word of God is also superior to the universal world, more ancient and general than all creatures. But his Angel, who is the Word, is represented as the Physician of our diseases, and that very naturally.' 'As the darkness vanishes at the rising of the light, and everything is enlightened, just so it is where the Divine

Word illuminates the soul.' Another Alexandrian Jew likewise speaks of the 'All-powerful WORD as the agent in the world's creation, as the guide and healer of the children of Israel in their wilderness journey, and the destroyer of the first-born of their oppressors.' All that there was of truth in this remarkable language of the Alexandrians, St. John seems to gather up in opening this passage of his Gospel, and to apply to Christ the Saviour. In this passage he seems to say to the Gnostics that true it was, as they asserted, there was a Word, but to affirm that this Word was in the beginning, that the Word was God, and that all things were made by him, each of which truths was a refutation of part of the Gnostic scheme of doctrine. And lastly, this passage of St. John seems to challenge and appropriate to the despised and crucified Jew, all these dark and half-understood sayings of the Grecian philosophers, in which they had spoken of a Word—sometimes as the Supreme reason and Guide of Man, sometimes as the Spirit and Ruler of the World."—*Barnes on St. John.*

"Heathendom was not without its 'unconscious prophecies,' and of its bards and philosophers it has been said, with no less truth than beauty, as 'little children lisp and tell of heaven, so thoughts beyond their thoughts to those high bards were given.' Again, it is scarcely, we think, to be supposed that St. John wrote what he did without some knowledge of and reference to Philo. So that, in this indirect way, we may with great probability, regard the language of the Greeks about the *Word* as illustrating the passage of the New Testament in which that epithet is applied to Christ."
—*Barnes, ibid.*

To the stoical writers, the name of the WORD was very familiar to express the Deity or all-pervading Soul of the World. This term was also used by the Jews as applicable to the Messiah. Thus, in their Targum on Deuteronomy xxvi. 17, 18, it is said:—"Ye have appointed the Word of God as king over you this day, that he may be your God." The term MIMRA, or THE WORD, was used by the Jews who were scattered among the Gentiles, and especially those who were conversant with the Greek philosophy.

THE INEFFABLE NAME. 63

The mind of man, indeed, seems bewildered and lost in contemplating the greatness of that Being, whose very name is wrapped up in impenetrable mystery. Josephus says, that the name was never known till the time that God told it to Moses in the wilderness, and that he himself did not dare to mention it, for that it was forbidden to be used, except once in the year, by the high-priest alone, when he appeared before the mercy-seat on the day of expiation. He adds, that it was lost through the wickedness of man; and hence has arisen a difference of opinion—some supposing the word itself lost, others the import or meaning only, and many the manner of delivery only, and the latter contend that Moses did not ask the Almighty for his name to carry to his brethren, but only for the true delivery or pronunciation. It is certain that the true mode of delivery cannot now be proved from any written record: 1st, because it is capable of so many variations from the manner of annexing the Masoretic points, which points were not extant in the days of Moses; and 2ndly, because the language now in use among the Jews is so corrupt and altered from that in which Moses wrote, that none of them—except a few of the very learned—understood anything of it, for which reason the Jews call it SHEM EMMURETH—the Unutterable Word. Philo tells us not only that the word was lost, but also the time, and the reason for the loss. But amidst all these learned disputes, one thing is clear, namely, that the NAME or WORD is expressive of SELF-EXISTENCE AND ETERNITY, and that this title can be applicable only to that Great Being who WAS, and IS, and EVER WILL BE.

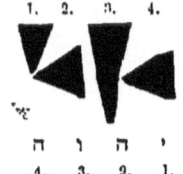

This figure is composed of four letters, and represents יהוה Jehovah. It frequently occurs on the slabs found at Nineveh. May it not be the famous quarternion or the Tetragrammaton of Pythagoras? The Jews were afraid the heathens would get possession of the name of Jehovah, and therefore in their copies of the Scriptures they wrote it in the Samaritan character instead of in the ancient Hebrew or Chaldee. They believed it, moreover, capable of working miracles, and they held that the wonders in Egypt were performed by Moses, in virtue of this name being engraven on his rod; and that any person, who knew the true pronunciation would be able to do all that Moses did. It was commanded in the Jewish law, that sentences from the Scriptures should be inscribed on the door-posts of their dwellings, and therefore the Jews had a custom of writing the Decalogue on a square piece of parchment, which they rolled up and put into a case, and after inscribing the name of God within a circle on the outside, they affixed it to the door-posts of their houses or apartments, and considered it a talisman of safety.

CHAPTER V.

Recapitulation of the four preceding chapters—Author's system more fully described—Antagonistic to all other theories—Sir H. Rawlinson's conjectures, and Author's translation of an inscription found upon a brick—A new hypothesis—Sir H. Rawlinson's Nineveh—The Author's translation—Mr. Layard's Sargon—The Author's translation—Ancient inscriptions in support of the new hypothesis—Remarkable coincidences between guesses and the Author's translations.

IN the preceding chapters, I have endeavoured to show that letters were the gift of God, and that the primitive language is the Hebrew tongue in all its essential points. I have stated my reasons for supposing letters to have been copied by Cadmus from Nineveh; that the most ancient written documents have been handed down to us in an alphabet remarkable for its brevity; that Moses wrote in the cuneiform character; and that this character is the earliest of all. I have given the history of the alphabet, and have shown that its formation is in strict accordance not only with the symbols used for the Divine Trinity, but also with a system of triads in use throughout the ancient world. I shall now proceed to enter a little more fully into the ancient system of writing.

It is acknowledged by all the Assyrian philologists that the cuneiform writing is from left to right. The groups of characters which Rawlinson calls letters are each composed of from two to five elements; but according to my system each element is a letter, and has its own individual phonetic power. Thus, referring to Rawlinson's Alphabet No. 1, (Plate 8.) we find that the first letter is composed of four elements, one placed horizontally over three perpendicular ones; but on looking at the primitive alphabet we see that the four elements change themselves into two primitive

F

letters, L and M, L being placed over M, Lm, or Lam, which word in the Persian language signifies "mercy, forgiveness," &c. Again, Rawlinson's, second letter B (No. 21,) is composed of three elements, and in the primitive alphabet it has also three, but it is two letters, B and Vau (Nos. 2 and 6)—Vau with the phonetic power of *ou*-Bou, signifying, "to go in and out," or "to reign." And so on through the whole alphabet, every Rawlinsonian letter resolving itself into a Persian, Arabic, or Hebrew word. Some persons may object to this system as being too complicated, for many of the groups have from ten to thirteen elements, and the numerals have even more; but then many of our own English words are composed of fourteen or sixteen letters. Then, to account for some of the letters being placed one over the other (see Plate V., No. 6, figure 2, and No. 5, figure 3), we must recollect that in the very earliest times stone was the only material used to write upon, and consequently the scribes would be very economical of space. We find this to be the case, for example, with the Lameds, which are sometimes double and sometimes treble. For instance, if we take the eighth letter in Rawlinson's alphabet, and place the elements in that cluster one after the other, we see what large space is required (Plate III., figure 1), and the consequent necessity for condensing them by placing them one above another. The group just referred to forms, according to my system, the word GAALL, "to redeem or buy back." I generally take the elements or letters in order, beginning at the top where there is more than one Lamed; but sometimes the word begins with L, and then the next or second letter will be over the L to the left, and the succeeding letters following on to the right (as in Plate III., figure 2). Sometimes the double L will be preceded by a letter, say Gimel or G, and then, from its peculiar figure, it will embrace both the upper and lower L and form the word GLL, "to roll over and over." (Plate III., figure 3.) Sometimes the upper L stands alone, and the lower will have a letter above on the left if there are more than one; or, if only one, it will be in the centre of the lower L (Plate III., figure 4); and in that case I take the upper L to be the preposition "to," and the lower, the word LN, "to dwell or abide."

As the reader will now, I hope, understand my method of reading the inscriptions, I shall proceed to give the results of the application of my alphabet to the Cuneiatic writing.

There is an inscription upon a brick (see Plate IV.), which Sir H. Rawlinson reads doubtfully as LEVEKH, the name of a city, which he supposes to be the *Calneh* of Genesis, or the *Halah* of Kings. He says: "The form is one, unfortunately, regarding which I entertain some *doubt;* its complete syllabic power is, I *think*, L-V, or, which would be same thing, in Assyrian R-M; but it also appears very frequently to represent one of these sounds, and whether this curtailment may be the effect of that resolution of the syllable into its component natural powers to which I have alluded, or whether it may be owing to the homogenity of the L and V, is a point which *I cannot yet venture to decide.* Such, indeed, is the laxity of expression in Assyrian, that even if the true power of No. 3, Plate IV., were proved to be L-V, I could still understand Nos. 3 and 4, Plate IV., being pronounced Halukh." I shall make no comment upon the above, but as this is the first inscription I attempted after I suspected the language to be Hebrew, I shall submit it to the opinion of those who may possibly be better acquainted with the Hebrew language than myself. The Hebrew scholar will perceive that there is, in my interpretation, no arbitrary distorting of the meaning, no substitution of ideas for sounds, no mystical homophones or ideographs, but a simple following out of the principle subsequently (though imperfectly) adopted by the Rev. C. Forster, the principle, namely, of giving to known alphabetical forms the same known alphabetical powers. With this key I found the inscription to read thus: "Thy son will be built up like a rock." By referring to Plate IV., the reader will find the groups in the Hebrew, Assyrian, and Cadmean numbered 1, 2, 3, 4; and by comparing the Assyrian with the Cadmean, or the second and third line of groups, he will see the principle of " like forms with like powers" carried out. I will subject this inscription to a critical analysis, in order to convince the reader of its truth and simplicity. I will take the groups in order: בנ‎ בן‎, the root of בנה‎ (BNE) with a radical, but mutable or omissible ה‎ (E) "to build up," &c., and also "the young," as the son is built up by his father, and the son also builds up and continues his father's house; of inanimate things it denotes what comes or is produced from another, for instance, a twig growing from the tree, is called in the Hebrew language, "the son of a tree;" the arrow shot from the bow is called "the son of the bow" and in this case, a brick is produced from clay, clay is the material to be *built up* or made into a brick, and as clay cannot be a brick until it has undergone certain changes of form, and is subjected to baking, burning, or exposure to the sun, therefore בנ‎ group 1st, בן‎ with the suffix כ‎, K "thy," will be "thy son." Group 2: Awleph or A denotes the first person singular, future; but as I have used it in the *third person*, a few words are necessary by way of explanation of this change. There is no doubt but that this brick inscription was written many centuries before the forma‑ tion of any system of Hebrew Grammar. Now, we find that Grammar grew up in the schools of the Greek philosophers; Plato had only two parts of speech (the noun and verb), and Aristotle added conjunctions and articles, but in his time there were not yet any such terms as singular and plural. About 250 years B.C. all pronouns were classed as articles; and even so late as in our own day Gesenius, the greatest of Hebrew grammarians, says that the "greatest difficulty is found in *the explanation of the third person.*" From all this I infer that in the earliest ages, before any of the nice distinctions of grammar were known, and before any attention was paid to syntactical arrangement, that the first and third persons were synonymous. To proceed:—Awleph, third pers., sing., future "it," is‎ (is), from ישה‎, a root unused in Hebrew, but found very widely spread in ancient languages, whence the noun יש‎ (esse), "being," and hence "to be,"—future "*will be*" (בן‎, BN) "*built up, made, or become.*" כ‎ (K), a prefix particle of similitude, "like;" צר‎ (TSR), "rock or flint,"="Thy son will be built up like rock." And this rendering is quite in accordance with what Herodotus tells us, in his description of Babylon, that the bricks, soon after they are made, become as hard as stone or flint.

The Rawlinsons, Layard, and others, imagine that most, if not all the inscriptions found on bricks consist either of the names of cities or of kings, and it so happens that the majority of the names actually thus discovered are those of well-known persons in sacred or profane history. Now, systems of decipherment which profess to recover names of kings, cities, and events previously known from Scripture or from ancient authors, naturally give rise to much doubt, for, as Mr. Forster justly remarks, the natural bent of most men engaged in such pursuits is to *find what they seek*, and to *see what they look for*.

From the experience I have had in deciphering the ancient Hebrew inscriptions found upon bricks, I venture to start the hypothesis, that the majority of the inscriptions found upon bricks are *not* the names of kings or cities, but are merely the passing thoughts of the brickmaker, stamped or marked down at a moment of leisure while the clay was soft. This could very easily be done with two sticks, the ends being made of a wedge shape (see Plate V., fig. 1), and with three sticks of this kind every combination or group could be formed.* The translations from various bricks, by means of the new alphabet, strongly favour this opinion. Take, for instance, the brick figured on Plate IV.:—"Thy son will be built up (made or become) like (to, or as solid as, a) rock." What can be conceived more natural than for the brickmaker, while thinking of the durable nature of the materials he was working up, to mark down at the moment his thoughts, with the tools he had by him for marking some important order? There is no doubt but that some bricks have been or will be found with names of kings or cities written upon them; but it

* In Rawlinson's "Five Ancient Monarchies," vol. i., I find the following remarkable statement corroborative of this suggestion :—"Tools with a triangular point made in ivory, apparently for cuneiform writing, have been found at Babylon."

is hardly reasonable to expect to find bricks inscribed with genealogical lists of kings. There is another inscription read by Sir H. Rawlinson as "Nineveh"—(see Plate V., fig. 2)—whether from a brick or not I cannot say; but from the fact that the sense eliminated is confirmatory of the new hypothesis, I should infer it was so. This inscription is composed of five groups of characters, consisting of twenty-one letters, forming nine words, according to the new theory; whereas Sir H. Rawlinson has but one word of seven letters. I will give the English with the Hebrew just as it occurs in the inscription, word for word and letter for letter, so that any Hebrew scholar can test its accuracy:—

"To rest,   nothing (so) desirable,   and   at the time (of)
 ללן   לה   ו   כ
 1.   2.   3.   5.
 refreshment always   to take   my log*   coming in."
 בלג   כל   בו   לגי   בו ؛
 6.   7.   8.   9.   10.

ללן לה או ו כ בלג כל בו לגי בו ؛
10. 9. 8. 7. 6. 5. 4. 3. 2. 1.

This translation may appear puerile, but I question whether it will not contrast favourably with the translations that invest every brick with an air of majesty, and that find on it names well known in sacred and profane history. Another inscription is expressive of the quality and destination of the object it is written upon:— "Thy gravelly and earthy matter will repair the roof and turrets, and make them smooth as stone." Another highly interesting inscription, supporting my hypothesis, is found on the Glass Vase, that beautiful and interesting relic of antiquity, discovered by Mr. Layard, and now in the British Museum. It is the earliest specimen of glassware in existence, and the inscription on it—(see Plate V., fig. 3)—is read by Mr. Layard as SARGON, the name of a king well-known in sacred history. Now, in this inscription there are seven groups, whilst in Layard's deciphered name there are

---

* There not being a word in the English language to express the exact meaning of the above word, I have retained the original, "Log," a Jewish measure of capacity containing three-quarters of a pint.

only six letters. By the application of the primitive alphabet we find it to consist of *ten* words, containing eighteen letters, and reading thus:—" Made round, expansive and transparent, for the purpose of (showing it) covers nothing secret.* Has not the second word in this inscription, CHUa (אנה), which, according to Gesenius, means " round, solid, compact, collected in itself," some reference to what Mr. Layard says in describing the vase:—That "it was originally cast in a solid piece, and afterwards drilled out, for the marks of the tools are plainly visible upon it?" This translation was made before I had seen " Nineveh and its Remains," or had known anything of the discovery beyond the fact that there was a glass vase found.

That the idea of engraving the thoughts of the maker upon

* As the reader may feel somewhat curious to know by what means Mr. Layard discovers the names upon bricks, &c., and as the method is not very intelligible, I will give his explanation *verbatim:*—"As the name of Sennacherib, as well as those of many kings, countries and cities, are not written phonetically, that is by letters having a certain alphabetical value, but by monograms, and the deciphering of them is a peculiar process which may sometimes *seem suspicious* to those not acquainted with the subject, a few words by way of explanation may be acceptable to my readers. The greater number of Assyrian proper names with which we are acquainted, whether Royal or not, appear to have been made up of the name, epithet, or title of one of the national deities and of a second word, such as 'slave of,' 'servant of,' 'beloved of,' 'protected by,' &c.—(this is nothing new; it is the same with many names in the Holy Scriptures)—like the Theodosius and Theodorus of the Greeks—(and he might have said like the 'Israel, 'Abimelech,' and 'Daniel,' of the Hebrews)—and 'Abd-ullah' and 'Able-un-rahman,' of the Mahommedan nations. The names of the gods being commonly written with a monogram, the first step in deciphering is to know which god this particular sign denotes. Thus, in the name Sennacherib we have the determinative of 'God,' to which *no phonetic value is attached:* whilst the second character denotes an Assyrian god, whose name was 'San.' The first component part of the name Essarhaddon is the monogram for the god Asshur. It is this fact which renders it *so difficult to determine with any degree of certainty or confidence* most of the Assyrian names, and which leads me to warn my readers, that with the exception of such as can be with certainty identified—(have the Assyrian Philologists identified a single name with certainty? no!)—with well-known historical kings, as Sargon, Sennacherib, and Essarhaddon, the interpretation of all those which are found upon the monuments of Nineveh is liable to *very considerable doubt.*"—Layard's "Nineveh," cap. vi., page 147.

articles of manufacture is quite in accordance with the custom of the ancients, can be proved from many inscriptions upon Greek and Etruscan vases, and other fictile ornaments, evidently copied from their more ancient neighbours the Assyrians. There are many antique vases in the museums in Europe with sentences and often colloquies written on them. Thus, on a vase on which the contest of Heracles and Cycnus is depicted, the hero and his opponent are made respectively to exclaim, "ΚΑΘΙΕ," "*lie down*," and "ΚΕΟΜΑΙ," "*I am ready*." On another, where Silenus is depicted gloating over his wine, he exclaims "ΗΔΥΣ-ΟΙΝΟΣ," "*the wine is sweet*," or "ΚΑΛΕ ΟΠΟΣ ΠΙΕΣΘΕ," "*it is so good that you may drink it*." Another vase has an inscription which bears no immediate reference to the vase itself, or to anything that it might be supposed to contain—a cock is represented in the act of crowing, with the words "ΠΡΟΣΑΓΟΡΕΥΟ," "*How d'ye do?*" Again, on a prize vase at Athens was inscribed "ΤΟΝ ΑΘΕΝΕΘΕΝ ΑΘΛΟΝ," "*I am a prize from Athens.*"

It is particularly gratifying to find some remarkable coincidences between the conjectures of some of the Assyrian philologists, and words I have found by means of the new alphabet. Amongst them all there is none so striking as the first five groups of characters of an inscription I brought with me from England. They were the first five words I construed by means of the Hebrew language, and the discovery encouraged me to proceed with the study of that tongue. I find that these first five words or groups are found upon all the slabs in the earliest palace at Nimroud, and hence Sir H. Rawlinson and others call it the standard inscription. (See Plate IV., fig. 3.) Mr. Layard, in his "Nineveh and its Remains," says, in a note, "It has been *conjectured* that the two first groups mean, *Palace or great house*." Now, mark the coincidence. The first group, according to the primitive alphabet, is Bmo (במו), without the masculine termination, signifying, "fortress," "castle," or "palace;" and the second word, CHU (חו), "to show, declare, or proclaim,"—Proclamation! The next character is the primitive Vau, which means "*together with*," "*and*." Then follow the last three groups, which read AASHOIK. The whole inscription is thus: "Proclamation—Palace and Aashoik." The coincidence here is the more remarkable as the application of the new alphabet was made before I had seen Layard's book, or knew anything of the locality of the mounds of Nimroud; for I find that the name "*Aashoik*" is preserved to this day in the mound immediately adjoining Nimroud — BAASHEIKah,—with the prefix B, and termination ah in addition, which is the modern orthography of the word. Again, in the fourth group (or Aash) Sir H. Rawlinson gives it as *Asshur*, and Dr. Hinckes is convinced that it is either that name, or an abbreviation of the name *Athur*, the country of Assyria. In another place he assigns to it the value of *tha*, and to the latter portion of it he gives the syllabic power of *Sa*. He also admits that group 4 (*Aash*), stands for the name of the city of which the historical name is *Nineveh*. But let us add group 5 to it, and we have at once the name which is still preserved in the supposed neighbourhood of Nineveh, namely, AASHOIK. Dr. Hinckes also imagines that the same group has the phonetic power of Sha. Sir H. Rawlinson identifies the groups 4 and 5, as Nineveh. These are significant coincidences, all pointing to what appears to be the true name of ancient Nineveh. Solomon truly says, "There is nothing new under the sun, and that which hath been is now," for we find our own beloved Queen adopting the very same kind of formula as that used 4000 years ago by Assyria's early monarchs, viz. :— "Proclamation! Buckingham Palace," or "St. James's Palace," or "Windsor Castle," as the case may be. What is the inference to be drawn from this striking coincidence and the simpler translation? Clearly, that the fact of these five groups of characters commencing every inscription in this particular saloon, with the more than probable meaning elicited by means of the new alphabet, amounts almost to absolute proof that the subject matter of each slab contains proclamations, edicts, or laws emanating from this particular palace of Aashoik. The slab from which the above inscription was taken bears a representation of a winged figure, or an Assyrian priest, carrying on his left arm a kid of the *Capræ Egagrus*, or Assyrian goat; in his right hand, held up, is something that bears a resemblance to an ear of corn; and the figure evidently appears to be about offering a sacrifice. The subject matter that follows the standard inscription is a prophecy of the destruction of the city, and an earnest prayer to the god 'Bel for enlightenment of mind, in words like these :—" Li, riz ou ecber rib tsr aluf; Beli, Beli, li bi, chu alu"—" Oh, that thou wouldst cry aloud and scatter the multitude of rock gods! My god, my god, oh that thou wouldst, show me the true god!" There is also an allusion to the destruction of the city of Baalbeg, destroyed through its crimes and gross depravity, though equal in splendour to Aashoik. This is the substance of the first four lines (very much abridged), containing more than 200 words. What volumes of ancient lore are yet locked up in the 20,000 sepharim already discovered, waiting for the true key to unlock this vast store of primitive literature! Well may Sir H. Rawlinson declare, that after all that has been done, that a beginning had only been made, and that Assyrian decipherment is only in its infancy.

CHAPTER VI.

The Sun worshipped in Assyria under the form of a Bull—Inscription found on the back of a winged Bull—Author's discovery of the Numerals on the Black Marble Obelisk—Annals of Aalpharr Rawlinson's Temen Bar. Rawlinson's errors in his numerals—Inscriptions on two marble Ducks. Singular coincidences between the Author's theory and the conjectures of Sir H. Rawlinson and others—Critical notice of the Rev. C. Forster's theory.

THERE is no doubt that the gods of the heathen were the heavenly bodies; but it is equally certain that they worshipped these bodies in conjunction with certain mortal creations. Thus, the Assyrians worshipped the sun, as being the most glorious body in the visible creation :—

"That with surpassing glory crown'd looked from his sole dominion,
As the God of this new world."

Under the symbolic form of the winged human headed bull, they gave expression to his attributes, of which tradition had spoken darkly. The human head was the type of intellect and knowledge, or of Omniscience; the body of the bull was the symbol of strength and power, or of Omnipotence; and the wings of the eagle were symbolical of ubiquity or Omnipresence. These winged bulls are thus no idle creations, no mere images of fancy. They have instructed races of men that have passed away more than 3000 years, and now they speak to us again in language equalled only by the inspired voice of Isaiah. The following is a translation from an inscription on the back of one of these winged bulls:—" Made to represent the supreme God." "I am Almighty, dwelling in heaven's circle, revolving and re-revolving the vast expanse in, who fails not in illuminating heaven's mysterious fires (whose), going out is nothing to equal the splendour of his coming return." *

There has been in the course of this work frequent allusions to the Assyrian numerals; the reader will very naturally ask by what means I arrive at a knowledge of them? The answer to this question will lead me to the relation of what I deem an important discovery in connection with the inscriptions on the Black Marble Obelisk. In the month of October, 1862, I formed the resolution of giving my version of the inscriptions on the Black Marble Obelisk, and in order to facilitate the work, I began forming a vocabulary or lexicon of every word found upon the monument (from the folio volume of inscriptions published by the authorities of the British Museum, under the superintendence of Sir H. Rawlinson), with its corresponding word in Hebrew or Arabic with its English meaning. Whilst prosecuting this work a certain group of characters or elements would obtrude themselves, of which I could make nothing: it was the fifth in consecutive order of the numerals (Plate IX.), which, as will be perceived, is composed of five separate elements. Now, had the three upper ones been joined together they would have formed the primitive letter M, and the two lower elements would similarly have made the letter N. I was inclined at first to give the group the phonetic value of Min, but I did not record it as a word. I next came upon the sixth character in the Plate, with the six elements all distinct. This led me to think that there was more meaning in them than I was aware of at that time. I observed that these two groups were preceded by a single character or element, the *Awleph* of the primitive alphabet, and followed by a group of six elements, but alike in both cases. I followed up the clue thus obtained, and Plate IX. will show the result of my discovery. At the time I made this discovery I was not aware that Sir H. Rawlinson had discovered any numerals, but upon subsequently perusing some of the Asiatic

---

* I regret that the foregoing translation was not finished in time for the lithographer, or I would have given the original inscription with the Hebrew words that it might be tested by the Hebrew scholar; should the work reach a second edition, I will give it with many additions.

AUTHOR'S DISCOVERY OF THE NUMERALS. 77

journals I saw that he had either discovered them, or by some singular coincidence, had given the exact number of years in the total of the reign of his supposititious Temen Bar II. Sir H. Rawlinson could not have known the groups referred to were numerals, for he tells us that the first fourteen lines are taken up with an invocation to the Assyrian gods, and he does not tell us there is any other matter between the invocation and the first year's annals of Temen Bar ; but immediately following the invocation he goes on to interpret thus :—" In the first year of my reign I crossed the Upper Euphrates," &c.,—thus leaving us to infer that the annals of the king commences on the fifteenth or sixteenth line. Now it may be stated confidently, that the annals of the king (whoever he may be) does not commence until nearly the close of the twenty-sixth line. (Dr. Hinckes says they commence on the twenty-second line.) Again, Sir H. Rawlinson, after giving the annals and the numerals in consecutive order (with the exception of the IV. year), up to the XX. year, instead of giving the XXI., XXII. and XXIII., he gives the XI., XII. and XIII. over again. (*Vide* Plate IX.) Now, on referring to Layard's "Monuments of Nineveh," we find them in the order they should be (XXI., XXII. and XXIII.) Sir H. Rawlinson proceeds rightly again until he comes to the XXIX. year, and there he gives the numeral XXVI. in its place; but upon referring to Layard's "Monuments," we find that there is *no numeral at all to be found*, the edge of the obelisk being so broken that the numeral is quite obliterated. The last three errors I look upon as almost proof positive that Sir H. Rawlinson did not certainly know those particular groups to be numerals, else he could have easily supplied the proper ones, as I have done. We can only come to the conclusion that Sir H. Rawlinson was ignorant of these particular groups being numerals, or was very careless in his supervision. It appears to me that he has made his imperfect knowledge of the numerals the sole foundation of his translations from the Black Marble Obelisk ; for wherever he finds a numeral he reads it as " so many times crossed the Euphrates," or " so many cities taken or burnt," or " so many captives taken or killed," &c. The numerals are the skeleton upon which he builds up the body of his translation; and the very fact of the numerals being composed of from *one* to *nine* elements, each element having *its own individual value*, must be subversive of his fanciful alphabet, in which there are from *one* to *nine* elements to form an individual letter. But more of this in its proper place.

To proceed with my discoveries respecting the numerals, I found that the numerals were preceded by a single character representing the *Awleph*, the initial of the article "*the*," and the first numeral followed by a group representing ASAS, which in Arabic means "principium rei," or "the beginning of a thing." Then the group of six elements, read by the primitive alphabet, are "AALFRR;" and the following group tested by the same means will give BKU with the suffix K, which means "thine by right of birth." The second year's annals begin with "The second (year) of thy reign AALFRR." Then follows a group which means "supreme king;" and then the group "thine by right of birth." Read collectively, it is "The second (*year* supplied) of thy reign AALFRR, supreme king, thine by right of birth." Then follow the annals of the year. And the annals of every succeeding year are preceded by the words translated above. Who is this AALFRR? I think he is to be identified as the Ballipares of profane history—Allipar or Aalfarr, with the modern prefix *B*, and the Greek termination, *es*—who was contemporaneous with Gideon, and whose name occurs frequently on the monument. From what has been said I infer that the annals on this interesting monument are not the annals of Temen Bar (who must have been one of the last kings of Assyria), but the annals of Aalpharr, the contemporary of Gideon.

The subject of the numerals has revealed two very interesting translations of small inscriptions found upon two marble ducks. These ducks are supposed to have been used as weights, and I have not read of any attempt having been made to elucidate the inscriptions on them: an attempt to do so by means of the primitive alphabet could not elicit any thing that I considered satisfactory, until I discovered the numerals, and then the reading appeared plain. The first inscription on the duck (marked G, figure 4, plate V.,) consists of eight elements which represent the numeral VIII., and two characters, Gimel and Vau, or G or K and ou—"Gou" or "Kou." "Gou," according to the Hebrew, is "the back, the middle, or the body." I think this duck was the representative of eight individual bodies called Gou or Kou (גב), a measure of length, as a measuring line. It is not at all improbable that in these times the term "Kou" was applicable both to measures of extension, and measures of weight; thus, the inscription on this duck would be descriptive of its weight "*eight gou*,"—as we would say, eight pounds. The duck (marked H, figure 5) appears to be a companion of duck G, and of the same weight, but differently expressed. The inscription is composed all of numerals excepting the middle character, *Awleph*, which is the article in the genitive case ("of the"), and it will read, "one-fourth of the thirty-second." The numerals expressive of the thirty-second are also alphabetical characters,— Gimel or G commuted for K (K, K, KN ; Kh, Kh, Khan), which, in Arabic, means an "Emperor" or "Monarch." Khan is a term used in the East to this day, as the Khan of Tartary. Now, may not this term have been used similarly to our "sovereign," the piece of money equal to twenty shillings ? We have also another piece of coin with an inscription which is quite analogous,—"one florin,"—and on the reverse "*one-tenth of a pound.*" I conclude, therefore, that the above inscription means "one-fourth of a Khan," or "Monarch," as well as "one-fourth of the thirty-second," which is equal to eight Kou or Gou, the weight of the duck marked G.

There appears to be a difference of opinion between Sir H. Rawlinson and Dr. Hinckes with respect to the numerals. The latter takes Sir H. Rawlinson's "bar" and "pal'" (Plate VI., figure 3) for his numeral VII., giving the vertical wedge (my Vau) the numerical power of V., and when placed to the left of a decade the power of L. (figure 4). In all other respects their numerals are essentially the same, only differently grouped. This same figure (figure 3) Rawlinson says, " certainly represents phonetically an Awleph א,

but it is also the ideograph for 'a son,' and in that capacity must, I think, be sounded 'bar,' and in the name of Sardanapalus we must give the sign in question the pronunciation of 'pal.'" (R.A.S., Vol. XII., page 405.) Here we have a simple group with five different powers, all as opposite to each other as possible—a letter, an ideograph for a word, a phonograph for the same word and of the same meaning, a phonetic syllable in a long name, and lastly the numeral VII.!

But, leaving these inconsistencies and contradictions, I turn to page 406 of the 12th volume, where I find Rawlinson says the figure (figure 5, plate VI.) "stands for sut." Now it will be observed that the same figure is the primitive S, the initial of sut. But then again he says that "figure 6 also stands for sut!" There is another singular coincidence worth mentioning. Sir H. Rawlinson, speaking of a certain group of characters, says (Plate VI., figure 2) that "in the ordinary Chaldean titles it seems to constitute a distinctive epithet;" but he cannot depend on its phonetic power. Now this distinctive epithet I find to be the name of a chief who figured in the wars against Gillirri, the supreme king. This name, Ausz ts,(6) occurs three times in the four gradines of the Black Marble Obelisk. On the second step from the top, face A, occurs this expression (according to my reading): "Ausz(6) ts fought fearfully, 1.2.3.4. 5. to prevent the entering of Aram (figure 1); I confined him 1.2.3.4. securely," &c. Sir H. Rawlinson says that the name of Assyria does not occur in any of the inscriptions; but it is well-known that the name of "Aram" is given to many parts in the East, and this name (as seen in Plate VI., figure 1) occurs many times on the Black Marble Obelisk.

From what has been already said the reader will perceive that the theory now submitted to the public in this work, in the preceding chapters, is entirely antagonistic to all theories hitherto propounded upon this subject. The nearest approach to its principle (in words only) is that by the Rev. C. Forster, whose theory is "The application of known alphabetic powers to known

alphabetic forms." This was precisely the principle I adopted ten years before Mr. Forster's book was published. Let us take one or two specimens of his translations to see how far his principle of " like known forms with like known powers" can be carried out.
1. Mr. Forster finds a slab, subject, "A Castle taken by Assault." Over it there is a short inscription (Plate II., figure 2). He says: " On my *first* glance at the inscription I observed a word (Plate II., figure 1), the *second* as read by me, and which I read Dab or Dabab." He goes on to state that "the inscription over it is brief, containing only five words, but the evidence supplied by one of these words (the first deciphered) outweighs volumes of learned conjecture." But why not give the first he deciphered? On his first glance he takes two letters (see Plate II., figure 2 marked with an asterisk) from two different groups which he renders according to the Arabic Dab or Dabab. Let any unprejudiced reader look at Mr. Forster's alphabet, and say whether there is the least likeness between the Hamyaritic B or D. and the characters he has picked out as " like known alphabetical forms with like known alphabetical powers." He next looks into Golius for the root, and he finds the following definition " dababat, an engine of war—a kind of battering ram ;" *then* he turns to the slab (which he had forgotten to examine) and finds pictured before him the whole definition: the murculus or rolling tower, filled with armed soldiers, and with a battering ram. He goes on to say, " The remaining words are equally clear," but he does not give us the words. The Rev. C. Forster is clearly as much at sea as he asserts the Messrs. Rawlinson and Layard to be. Would it not have been more satisfactory for Mr. Forster to have taken the inscription word by word, and to have given something like a connected and reasonable interpretation, than to have cut out a part of two different words, and give them an arbitrary meaning to suit the device, and then to sum all up in this grandiloquent style :—" It would be difficult to find a legend so comprehensively explanatory of its device as this single word." I perfectly agree in the principle laid down, and believe it to be the only safe rule ; but why does not Mr. Forster

consistently follow it out? Let us take another specimen of this gentleman's abilities as a decipherer of the Assyrian cuneiform. He then commences with that highly-interesting monument of antiquity, the Black Marble Obelisk; and after freely commenting upon what Sir H. Rawlinson has done in the way of deciphering it, he proceeds to give us his own views upon the subject, grounded on the principle of "Legend and device, and like powers and like forms." Now, this monument or obelisk has four sides, and, according to Sir H. Rawlinson's classification they are marked A, B, C and D, and there are five series of figures—men and animals running round the four sides. Under each series of figures there is an inscription in the cuneiform character, which is called an epigraph, consequently there are five epigraphs. Mr. Forster, it seems, contrary to the opinions of all the Assyrian philologists, reads the cuneiform from right to left. In the first series of figures on side C, in the right hand corner, is seen a figure bearing on his head a kind of tray, containing what appear to be fruits of the earth—water-melons or something very much like them; and immediately under this figure, in the second series, is a similar object, carrying another tray with articles resembling our modern one-pound bundles of cigars.* There is also another figure in the fifth series, side A, bearing a similar tray to those on side C. Mr. Forster casts about him to find a word that will suit the figures of his choice, but there is no word that will suit the device in the first, second, or third epigraphs, excepting at the conclusion of each epigraph, which occurs on the last side D. In the fourth epigraph to the left of face C he finds a word that seems to answer his purpose (see Plate III. A, fig. 1.,) which he applies to the first figure to the right in the first series. This he translates from the Arabic, "Dar—

* It may be as well to observe here, for the information of those who have not seen this interesting relic of antiquity, that the five series of figures appear to illustrate the tribute or conciliatory gifts from the king or chief of some distant country, for they consist of animals (tame and wild,) minerals, precious woods, vases, textile fabrics, and what appear to be the products of the earth, which are borne by sixty attendants and their officers to the king, who is seen in the first and second series, side A.

a paunch." Then he applies it to the first figure to the right in the second series, and calls that also "Dar—honeycomb tripe." In the fifth epigraph, the word occurs three times, but in no instance is the group or legend under the device. Indeed, the legend is so far from the device, that no reasonable being could suppose there ever was any connection between them. With this arbitrary system of deciphering them, Mr. Forster says that the second figure is carrying "honeycomb tripe," and the first bearing "paunches uncut," consequently, unclean! He also gives this word five different meanings, as opposite in idea as black to white. He finds it under a figure carrying something on his shoulder like an elephant's tusk, and he calls it, "Dar, dar; dentes defflui—shed teeth." He has also found three other groups, but very different from the fig. 5, which, he says (fig. 2), means "shed teeth." Then he finds it under a figure bearing a bag on his shoulder, and he gives it the name of grain, "dharoo—milii genus." Again, the same word is found, the last but three, at the end of each epigraph; and from its frequent repetition he gives it the signification of "*quod frequenter penditur tributum*—frequently paid tribute." If he had strictly followed out his own principle, the word would have had many more names equally opposite to each other. Thus, it occurs under a camel, under a baboon, under a figure bearing a bundle of sticks, and also under a figure carrying a skin of wine or some kind of liquor; for the leading figure of that series holds in his hand a glass or tumbler, and the one behind him has an open vessel, apparently to dip out of occasionally. But I think enough has been said of the "Legend and Device" principle to satisfy all candid readers of its uselessness. Let us now look at Mr. Forster's Alphabet to see how far the principle of "like forms with like powers" will act. In the example before us, it will be seen at a glance that there is not the slightest resemblance between No. 1 D or B and the Hamyaritic Plate II., or between the D's of Plate II. and III. In fact, the thing seems to be a mass of inconsistencies.

In Plate III., fig. 6, is the translation by means of the primitive alphabet, and fig. 7 is the four concluding words of each epigraph, with the rendering by means of the Hebrew language. I shall close this notice of Mr. Forster's works with an extract from his own book :—" It was prosecuting inquiries on the principle in question, *i.e.*, like alphabetical forms with like alphabetical powers, that I found its alphabet limited to ten letters, while it was by means of this alphabet that I obtained *all the results* hereafter to be mentioned, and to which I have here alluded only by anticipation, and the result of which was *most disappointing*. It was literally 'Parturiunt montes; nascitur ridiculus mus.' Yet so far it proved satisfactory, as demonstrating the invariable application in all these primitive pictorial monuments, of the principle of Legend and Device."

CHAPTER VII.

Sir H. Rawlinson's Assyrian Alphabet—Opinion of it, by Dr. Wall—Ideographs—Darkness visible—Rawlinson's method more fully explained—Discrepancy in the history of his Alphabets—His doubts—Rawlinson's translation of Temen Bar's brick—Coincidences: White is black, and Black is white—"Pote's Nineveh"—"Bonormi's Nineveh"—Bunsen's opinion of the system of Dr. Hinckes.

It must be clear to every person who has made the present subject in any degree a study, that the systems hitherto sent forth to the world in this particular branch of philology are far from conclusive or satisfactory. There seems to be a void,—a want of something more tangible than conjecture,—and this opinion is largely shared in by some of the most learned men of the present day, as will be seen in the sequel. Indeed, Sir H. Rawlinson confesses himself to be in a state of doubt from first to last, for he says:—" It would be disingenuous to slur over the broad fact, that the science of Assyrian decipherment is yet in its infancy: *a commencement has been made, and that is all.*" Dr. Wall, of Trinity College, Dublin, in his essay on the Rawlinsonian Alphabet, says:—" Surely such complicated characters, consisting of so many and such various ingredients, could not have been, in the first instance, applied to the expressing the simple elements of articulate sounds; it is quite inconceivable that they could; no alternative therefore seems left to us, but to conclude that it is mere waste of time and labour to attempt to analyse them by methods, in accordance with notions hitherto in vogue upon the subject."

Sir H. Rawlinson, again, in speaking of his alphabet of 150 letters and 500 variants, says:—" The alphabet is partly ideographic," (we are not quite sure what *Rawlinson can mean by this* term ideographic. We think the term, as applied to written characters, is only calculated to mystify the subject; therefore, better left alone,) "and sometimes syllabic; where a sign or letter represents a syllable, *I conjecture* that the syllable in question *may have been* the specific name of the object which the sign or letter was supposed to depict." (Thus: if א, A, Awleph, represents an "ox," and ב, B, Beth, a "house," therefore אב, AB, will be an "ox house," or a stall for cattle, instead of "father," &c. This appears to be the meaning according to the above system!) "Whilst in cases where a single alphabetical power appertains to the sign, *it would seem* as if that power had been the dominant sound in the name of the object. In this way, at any rate, are we alone *I think*, able to account for the anomalous condition of many of the Assyrian signs which sometimes represent phonetically a complete syllable, and sometimes one only of the sounds of which the syllable is composed." (The nearest approach to the first case is מֹ מִ Mím, "water," and in the second instance we have הא, hae, and פא, pae.) "It certainly cannot be maintained that the phonetic portion of the alphabet is altogether syllabic, or that every phonetic sign represents a complete and uniform articulation. The entire phonetic structure is thus shown to be in so rude and elementary a state as to defy the attempt to reduce it to any definite system. . . . A still more formidable difficulty, one indeed of which I can only *remotely conjecture* the explanation, is that certain characters represent two entirely dissimilar sounds—sounds so dissimilar that neither can they be brought into relation with each other, nor will the other power be found to enter at all into the full and original articulation. (Plate II., fig. 1.) In some respects the Assyrian alphabet (*i.e.*, Sir Henry Rawlinson's alphabet) is more difficult to be made out than the Egyptian. In the latter, the object depicted can always be recognised, and the Coptic name of the object will usually give in its initial form the phonetic power of the hieroglyph; whereas in Assyrian the machinery by which the power is evolved is *altogether obscure:* we neither know the object nor, *if we did know it, should we be able to ascertain its Assyrian name!* . . . The inscrip-

RAWLINSON'S METHOD EXPLAINED. 87

tions at Persepolis and Pasægadæ are almost in every instance trilingual and triliteral. They are engraved not only in three different languages, but the alphabets varying from each other not only in their elemental signs, but in their whole phonetic structure —the object of course being to render them generally intelligible. To this fashion, then, of triple publication are we indebted for our knowledge of the Assyrian inscriptions. By careful comparison of these duplicate forms of writing the same name, and other appreciation of the phonetic distinctions peculiar to the two languages, have been then supplied the means of determining with more or less certainty, the value of about 100 Babylonian characters; and a very excellent *basis* has been obtained for a complete arrangement of the alphabets. By mere comparison however, repeated in a multitude of instances so as to reduce almost infinitely the chance of error, I have added nearly fifty characters to the 100 which were previously known through the Persian key; and to this acquaintance with the phonetic value of 150 signs is, I believe, limited my present knowledge of the Babylonian and Assyrian alphabets." Limited! How many would Sir Henry Rawlinson have? But this is not all: the consonant sounds recognised in the Assyrian language are only sixteen, each consonant being capable of two combinations, and each combination having a different character, "as, ap, ip, up, pa, pi, pu." Consequently, this would give ninety-six different characters. It then proceeds into fresh combinations, and if carried out to its fullest extent it would give a list of between eight and nine hundred different characters! But certain phonetic laws (not to be arrived at) intervene to check this exuberant growth, and even then the known Assyrian alphabet is thus raised to between two hundred and forty and two hundred and fifty characters! Nor is this all. There are other characters, which are called "determinatives," to be prefixed to certain classes of words in order to determine their character. Thus, the single vertical wedge placed before a word tells us that that word is the name of a man, and the vertical wedge preceded by two horizontal wedges tells us to expect the name of a god. (It is a singular coincidence that the three characters just described, according to the primitive alphabet, mean "chief" and also "god.") Then, again, there are ideographs and monograms to swell the number nearly to three hundred, besides many more whose phonetic power is wholly unknown, yet they make this important confession, that the Assyrian language is *unmistakably Semitic* and bears *the closest relationship to the Hebrew.*

Professor Rawlinson, in his "Five Ancient Monarchies," assigns the original invention of letters to a period before the Hamite race had broken up and divided. He says:—"They adopted a system of picture-writing which aimed at the communication of ideas through the rude representation of natural objects, and belonged, as it would seem, not only to the tribes who descended the Nile from Ethiopia, but to those also who, perhaps diverging from the same focus, passed eastward to the valley of the Euphrates. The original pictures were reduced in process of time to characters for the convenience of sculpture, and these characters being assigned phonetic values, which corresponded with the names of the objects represented. There is sufficient evidence to show that the process of alphabetical formation was nearly similar to that which prevailed in Egypt. In particular it is true there is a marked difference in the respective employment of hieroglyphic and cuneiform characters: in the former alphabet each character has but one single value, while in the latter the variety of sounds which the same letter may be used to express is quite perplexing; but this discrepancy of alphabetic employment does not argue a diversity of origin for the system of writing, it merely indicates a difference of ethnological classification in the nations among whom the science of writing was developed, as the inhabitants of the valley of the Nile were essentially one nation and used but one vocabulary. The objects which the hieroglyphics represented were each known to the people of the country by one single name, and each hieroglyphic had thus one single value; but in the valley of the Euphrates the Hamite nation seems to have been broken up into a multitude of distinct tribes, who spoke languages identical or nearly identical in organisation and grammatical structure, but varying to a very great extent in vocabulary, and the consequence of this; that as there was but one picture alphabet common to the whole aggregate of tribes, each character had necessarily as many phonetic values as there were distinct names for the object which it represented among the different sections of the nation."

But is not this latter paragraph—" the wish which is father to the thought" of the Rawlinsonian theory—purely conjectural? Certain it is, that it is contrary to Scriptural facts. The Books of Moses are the only works we can refer to for events in those prehistoric times, and from them we learn that Abram went out from Ur of the Chaldees into Mesopotamia, dwelling amongst the Semitic and Hamitic tribes; that subsequently he went into Egypt, and from thence into Canaan, and dwelt amongst the *Oaks of Mamre* in the midst of the Hamite race, who, as we are told, were broken up into a multitude of distinct tribes, but who all spoke languages nearly identical in grammatical structure, having but one alphabet common to the whole, but each individual letter or character having as *many phonetic values* as there were distinct tribes, *i.e.* a multitude of values! How is it possible that Abram, Isaac, or Jacob, in their travels to and fro in the East, could understand such a jargon? It does not appear that there was any *bar* to that free intercourse of speech, which we naturally expect to find among a people who spoke the same language. In the early part of this work I have spoken on the universality of the primitive language, and of the non-dispersion of tongues, therefore I need not say any more upon that point here.

There is a discrepancy in Sir H. Rawlinson's history of his alphabet which I should like to see cleared up. In the Behustan or Persian alphabet he has forty letters (*vide* Plate VIII.,) and speaking of the Behustan inscriptions he says:—" They are engraved in three different languages, and *each language has its peculiar alphabet*, the alphabets indeed *varying from each other* not merely in the characters being formed by a different assortment of the elemental signs which we are accustomed to term the arrow-head or wedge, but in their whole phonetic structure and organisation." Further on he says:—"There is, therefore, no doubt but that the alphabets of Assyria, of Armenia, of Babylonia, of Susiana, and of Elymais are, as far as *essentials* are concerned, *one and the same.*" Now, by "essentials" Sir Henry Rawlinson cannot here mean the letters of the alphabet; he must mean the wedges or elements of which the letters are composed, and yet in some instances, where one or more of these wedges obtrude themselves uninvitedly, they are called *non-essentials!* According to his own account he has 150 letters in the Assyrian alphabet, with 500 variants; but his brother the professor, in the "Five Ancient Monarchies," doubles the number, and with this multitudinous alphabet they cannot translate a very simple inscription on a brick (see Plate IV.) I would ask—Has the development of the Assyrian cuneiform reached that point of perfection to justify the assertion, beyond dispute, that the *name of any particular king* has been stamped on a brick? I think not. All has been doubt and conjecture. We hear from him, the greatest of Assyrian philologists, such expressions as these—"I conjecture," "I read the two names doubtfully," "I cannot depend on its phonetic power," and lastly, "I will frankly confess indeed, that having mastered every Babylonian character, and every Babylonian word to which any clue existed in the trilingual tablets, either by direct evidence or by induction, I have been tempted on more occasions than one, in striving to apply the key thus obtained, to abandon the study altogether, in utter despair of arriving at any satisfactory result." What would be thought of a king in our day who would give utterance to such a rigmarole as Sir H. Rawlinson ascribes to Temen Bar, the great grandsire of Pul:—"Temen Bar, the great king, supreme and powerful king, king of Assyria, son of Assaradanapal, the great king, supreme and powerful king, king of Assyria, son of Abedbar, powerful king, king of the land of Assyria, of the city of Halah." Is it to be supposed for a moment that the king of a nation which had flourished for more than a thousand years,

—which had advanced in all the arts and sciences, and even in literature (as the voluminous nature of its records testify)—would adopt such a method of perpetuating the genealogy of his family, and that only for three generations? In this translation the word king occurs eight times, but the group which I suppose to be taken to mean "king" (Plate VI., fig. 7,) occurs ten times. Why I suppose this particular group to be so taken is because, in the *Asiatic Journal*, vol. xii., Sir H. Rawlinson says:— "The monogram (Plate VI., fig. 7,) which has the full power of "*Men*," may also possibly stand for "*Melek*,"—"King." Now, according to the primitive alphabet, we see this group representing the Hebrew word גג, GG, which means, "top, roof, cover, extent, or expanse, above," and where the stem letter is repeated, "supreme"—*i.e.*, above all. This shows a singular coincidence; for, in Parkhurst's Lexicon, article גג, GG, we find it stated that "to this root may be referred אגג, AGG, which appears to be the common name of the *Kings of the Amalekites*, from the comparatively *large extent* of their dominions." There are in this inscription forty-six groups of cuneatic characters, each containing from one to six elements or wedges. Now, according to his own theory, in which every group is a letter or monogram,—and allowing four letters to be the average of a word, or even allowing only one-half to be monograms or words, there would be far too few characters to warrant the above translation. Why does not Sir H. Rawlinson give us the language by which he translates, that we might the better test it? In fact, there is scarcely a name upon any of the bricks that is twice given alike. The groups upon one brick which he interprets as "Son of Abedbar," on another he interprets as "supreme and powerful king." Then, again, the groups which he at one time acknowledges to be the numeral, "M.," and the Number "8," he interprets at another time as being part of "King of the land of Assyria." Probably he would say they are "variants." *Numerals* variants of *words!*

But a word or two here on this system of variants. Mr. Layard says:—"I have already alluded to the laxity prevailing in the construction and orthography of the language of the Assyrian inscriptions, and to the number of distinct characters which appear to make up its alphabet. Letters differing widely in their forms, and evidently the most opposite in their phonetic powers, are interchangeable. The shortest name may be written in a variety of ways; every character in it may be changed till at last the word is so altered, that a person unacquainted with the process it has undergone, would never suspect *the two were in fact the same.*" Upon the very same principle we can *prove* that "BLACK is WHITE," by allowing W to be a "variant" of B; H of L; I of A; T of C; and E of K; *ergo*, they are *one and the same thing!* Mr. Layard goes on to say:—" By a careful comparison of inscriptions more than once repeated, it will be found that many characters, greatly or altogether differing in form, are only varieties or variants of the same letter." A very convenient method this, of solving difficulties! And it is by such improbable means these high authorities arrive at conclusions, quite opposite to sense and reason, and to all alphabetical systems ancient or modern! Indeed, Sir H. Rawlinson himself seems to be aware of this; for he says,— "The anomaly which cannot fail at first to attract the attention, and excite the astonishment of Orientalists is, that whilst all the Semitic alphabetical systems with which we are acquainted, are distinguished for their *rigour* and *compactness*, the primitive lapidary writing of the same races, occuping the same seats, should be constructed on a scale of such extraordinary amplitude and laxity." It would, indeed, be an extraordinary thing if it was so!

It is evident from the writings of these gentlemen that they are dubious as to the truth of their own theory. Mr. Layard says:— " From our present limited knowledge of the character used in the inscriptions, it would be hazardous to assign any positive date to the Palaces, or to ascribe their erection to any monarch; although a conjecture may be allowed, we can come to no positive conclusion upon the subject, *more progress is required in deciphering the character.*" And accordingly this self-evident uncertainty must extend itself to the professed interpretations of the language by means of their alphabet! But to proceed, "Our readers will see on what foundation rests the historical discoveries; the words without sounds (ideographs) we must either denounce as a *monstrous doctrine*, exposing distinctly that the reading or decipherment is yet in its infancy, or the want of a definite language the only ground on which this *startling theory* can be accepted for a moment."—(" Pote's Nineveh.") Again,—"The recoveries are too few, the developments consequently too incomplete in themselves, unfortunately, to satisfy the importunities of knowledge; a mythic form or monstrous combination, the figured veil of an unknown rite or mystic ceremonial, conceals the features that curiosity asks learning to trace in their truth. The world gazes on the disjected members and fossil bones of Assyrian antiquity, and calls vainly for science to array the scattered fragments into shape, and warm them into expression with the magic arts of divination. The shade has been evoked from its tomb; but where is the charm that shall compel its voice to reveal the buried secrets of the past? If the original system is incomplete and contradictory IT CANNOT ALL BE TRUE."—(*Ibid.*)

But if a new principle, while it solves all the difficulties of the consequences, reconciles and explains also all the contradictions we fancy or find in the original writers,—if, in fact, it arranges and simplifies all that we possess or can obtain of myth, tradition, or history, and can combine these into a general and, indeed, universal system, concordant with and even establishing some earlier portions of Holy Writ, we must perforce give it credence. This effort of reason will be duly recompensed: for she will then possess a calculus for every problem of antiquity; and all that has hitherto lain unknown or obscure in the general history of the world, will combine into a single channel, clear, bright, obvious, and demonstrative to the least reflective mind, while courting the sternest scrutiny of the widest research."—*Ibid.* "The great feats of interpretation which such a man as Sir H. Rawlinson has accomplished should not be suffered *to blind us to the fact* that our materials for Assyrian history, even now, after a partial elucidation of such inscriptions as have been found, are extremely limited and fragmentary, and in their present state convey *little that is positive in its results*, at least so far as chronological narrative is concerned. The system of Assyrian writing is extremely obscure, and the language which it records is only *partially intelligible through the imperfect key of the Behustan inscriptions."—Bonormi's Nineveh and Her Palaces.*

And what has been already said will apply equally to the system of Dr. Hinckes, Fox Talbot, and others, who work on the same principle. Bunsen, in speaking of the system of Hinckes, says:—" In one word, such a system may be admitted as one means of subjective *guessing;* but Dr. Hinckes will not expect that it should be recognised as a scientific method. The results of his own ingenious guesses have indeed *considerably varied*, and I believe few of them which were not already arrived at by Rawlinson will be found to be conclusive."

Thus we see, from the foregoing extracts, that what has been hitherto done in the way of elucidating those dark and mysterious writings is extremely doubtful and unsatisfactory, and that some new principle of interpretation is wanted, at once simple, clear, and intelligible.

CHAPTER VIII.

No Apology for the Contents of this Chapter—Author's Motive for Writing—
"Brandis" on the Assyrian Inscriptions and Mode of Decipherment—
Rawlinson's "I am Darius"—Author's Translation—Forster's Translation
of the same—Rawlinson's "Phraortes"—Author's Translation—Queries
respecting his Alphabet—Inconsistencies and Errors in Rawlinson's
Translation of the Black Marble Obelisk.

I DO not think it necessary to make any apology for the contents of this chapter, for the various works that have been written upon this occult subject are now before the world, and have become public property, and are therefore open to fair criticism. The subject, besides, is of too much importance to require an apology from me for speaking plainly my thoughts on the subject. The world has been in my opinion imposed upon by the rank and talent of literary men, who have confidently put forth statements on this subject, calculated to sap the very foundations of Biblical truth,—statements founded only on *baseless conjecture.* These pages have not been written for the mere sake of dissension, but from a sincere love of truth ;—not from love of antagonism, but to correct error.

This work has been written at leisure moments, not with any pecuniary motive, but with a sincere and fervent hope that it may meet the eye, and awaken the zeal of Oriental scholars, and induce them to give this new theory a fair and candid trial. If it shall happen to be accepted, "*Palmam qui meruit ferat;*" but, in any case, it has been carried on to completion with much patient study, and with the sincere prayer that it may tend to the further elucidation and confirmation of the Holy Scriptures.

I shall now proceed to give the opinions of several learned men on the schemes of interpretation adopted in the works of Rawlinson and others. And first, Brandis, in his work on "Assyrian Decipherment," says:—"In the remains of the Babylonian text of the Behustan inscriptions, which have unfortunately suffered from time and the weather, we have about 160 different characters. Rawlinson gives a list of 246 arrow-headed forms, which he has found partly in Assyrian and partly in Babylonian records. It is certain that this number might be increased (*ad infinitum*) by a comparison of all the Ninevite inscriptions. This variety becomes still greater in consequence of the multitude of variations in which these characters appear in the different inscriptions. If after ages might commiserate the Babylonians and Assyrians, for being obliged to use this multitude (as it would seem) of arbitrary forms, this pity must give place to speechless astonishment at the declaration of such men as Rawlinson and Hinckes, "*that the scholars of Mesopotamia may have used perhaps a fourth part of those figures for several sounds entirely different from each other.*" If such variations can be demonstrated our efforts to decipher them must certainly be in vain, and we shall be obliged not merely to wonder at the boldness of the Assyrians in daring to tolerate them, but much more at their ability to read their own writing. Next, so long as the phonetic value of the signs was adhered to, a series of words resisted all attempts to bring them into connection with any known language; and, finally, the great variety of variations in the names of the Assyrian kings, and in several other proper names, appeared to confirm his hypothesis. Once in possession of such a principle, *it was natural that the work of deciphering should go rapidly forwards,—no difficulty was so great as not to be, in this manner, happily solved.* A striking instance is furnished us in the teatment of the name of a king who styles himself Ruler of Assyria, and son of Sennacherib, and consequently can be no other than Assarhaddon. The first sign agrees with this, being the sign at Behustan to express the land of Assyria; and in the Ninevite inscriptions both this and the god Assar. But the last of the three characters which compose the name is the same as the first. From this difficulty Hinckes easily escapes—"The initial character is to be read Assar, but in the end of the name PERHAPS DON!" *Credat judeus apella.* Happily we are able to show that no such violence was necessary, for the full name of the Assyrian was Assar-don-Assar, *i.e.*, Assar, Lord of Assyria, and the abbreviated form was in use only among the people. Be this as it may, *the thing is so utterly incredible as to render any other mode of solving difficulties preferable to this.* Neither hieroglyphics nor alphabetic writing furnishes the least analogy to such *lawlessness.* Nor is the manner in which Rawlinson seeks to explain the origin of the alleged polythong at all satisfactory. We may admit without scruple that the cuneiform writing was originally derived from the hieroglyphic, although the phonetic part of the letter must have been at the time considerably developed, because in no other way can the use of generic signs before the names of persons, countries, rivers and the like be accounted for; but that in Mesopotamia, the figure of an object was employed for all its various names is opposed to all probability. Even in Egypt each figure retained always its distinct phonetic value; and where, as a generic sign, it appears to have lost this property, it was not pronounced. Accordingly, we believe that in a large number of ARROW GROUPS A DEFINITE CONVENTIONAL LAW OF FORMATION MAY BE TRACED. If this discovery be verified, it runs *directly counter, it is plain, to that theory.* Finally, our distrust of this lawlessness is still more increased by the fact that so many important parts of the Ninevite inscriptions can be deciphered without assigning to the individual cuneiform characters more than *one sound* which each has been proved to represent." Can anything be more prophetic of the theory shown in this work? One would almost imagine that M. Brandis had been gifted with the power of foreknowledge.

Secondly, in a letter from Mr. Fox Talbot, inserted in the "Journal of Sacred Literature," and in which he defends the Rawlinsonian system, he says:—" There exists at the same time in the minds of many a very considerable degree of doubt and hesitation with respect to the reality of the alleged discoveries.

This scepticism does not apply to the details merely, but extends to the very root and foundation of the whole system. Indeed, some writers have not hesitated to come forward in print and boldly aver their belief that *the whole thing is a delusion*, and that Sir H. Rawlinson and Dr. Hinckes have completely deceived, first themselves and then the world, with regard to a long series of statements of the highest historical and literary importance which they have confidently and repeatedly put forward." And I would ask, can anyone who has entered thoughtfully into the works of Sir H. Rawlinson, and have seen the numberless errors, inconsistencies, and arbitrary strainings he has had recourse to in his translations refuse to join in the sentiments just expressed? Let the reader follow me while I give a few examples. Rawlinson attempts his translations by means of an alphabet composed of the joint discoveries of Grotefend and other German and French scholars, who, with himself, have formed an alphabet of thirty-nine letters, and with what he calls a "disjunctive sign"—making a total of forty characters, besides a great number of variants. Each of these characters (as I have said before) is composed of from two to five elements; but not *one* of the various groups of elements is anything similar in figure to any ancient or modern letter. In the Primitive Alphabet each one of the elements becomes a letter; consequently, a Rawlinsonian letter forms a primitive word, as I shall now show by an example testing the truth of the primitive alphabet.

Believing that at one period of time there was only one cunciatic alphabet in use all over the East, and that the Persians were the last to use it, I resolved to test the Persian Behustan inscriptions, or rather, to test my alphabet by means of these writings. The beginning of the inscription, according to Rawlinson, is "Adam Darywush,"—"*I am Darius.*" Now, the first letter in this short sentence, in Rawlinson's alphabet (Plate VIII.,) is composed of four elements—one horizontal over three vertical wedges (Plate VI., fig. 8,) forming Rawlinson's A, but the primitive LM (*vide* Tablet of Alphabets) or Lam (meaning in Persian "mercy," "forgiveness," "tranquillity," and "rest.") The second is a similar group with two vertical wedges (fig. 9,) Rawlinson's D, and the primitive LN or Lan (in Persian an emphatic negative, "No! it shall not be that," "certainly never.") The third letter, A, is supplied. The fourth letter is composed of one short horizontal wedge and three vertical ones (two long and one short,) forming Rawlinson's M (fig. 10,) primitive A, ou i ou (Persian Awi, singular, "he, she it;" plural, Awiou, "they.") Collectively—Rawlinson's, "I AM;" primitive, "They shall not (find) mercy." D, A, same as before. The sixth letter, Rawlinson's R, is composed of three horizontal wedges (two long and one short) and one long vertical wedge, forming the primitive LALU (Persian, "a long, dark night, or time of affliction and sorrow:" Hebrew, LILI, לִיל, "night.") The seventh letter (fig. 14) is Rawlinson's Y, but the primitive Yaja, ("foolish words, vain, vagabond, or foolish fellow that knows not what he does,") used in this instance as "foolish." The eighth letter (fig. 15) composed of five elements, forms Rawlinson's W, primitive *Aoul* (Persian "*Awl*," race, offering, posterity, progeny, descendants, &c.) and "*Al*" the article, equal to *Awlal* "the race" (and this form used only when the race or family is *noble*.) The ninth letter (fig. 16,) Rawlinson's U, primitive *Gan*, or which is the same in Persian *Jan* ("life, soul, mind, vital spirit, self, wind, the mouth," &c.) The tenth and last letter is composed of three elements (fig. 17,) forming Rawlinson's SII, but the primitive *Lgg* or *Lkk* (Persian "imprisonment, pain, trouble, sorrow," &c.) Therefore the translation by means of the primitive alphabet will read thus:—"They shall not (find) mercy nor rest (during) a long time of adversity, the foolish race (but) imprisonment for life." This appears to be the middle of a speech, or an address to certain individuals, and the very attitude of the king (as represented on the Behustan rock) with his hand uplifted to the prisoners before him is indicative of the fact. And the word *Awlal* ("the race,") which is only applied to noblemen, is in the right place, if the prisoners are the nobles that conspired against the throne and life of Darius. It will not be out of place here to notice (to say the least of it) *the very curious* translation, by the

Rev. C. Forster of the same ten groups treated of above:—"A CUT SHORT MAN ENGRAVING MANY CAPTIVES FASTENED BY A SINGLE ROPE, BY CUTTING AND STRIKING WITH A MALLET." I shall let the reader judge between the three translations; the latter is certainly beneath criticism.

Encouraged by my apparent success with the above ten groups, I determined to test another small inscription from the Behustan rock. I selected the one cut upon the dress of the third standing figure to the right of the king, and continued on the rock beside it. Rawlinson says that these inscriptions are in *almost every instance triliteral;* but in the instance before us there are only *three* words that are triliteral, and he is obliged to supply one to each to make sense of it. In the whole inscription he supplies thirty-four letters, making a total of one hundred and five, whereas in the original (according to his own alphabet) there are only seventy-one, viz.:—" Iym frwrtish adhurujhiy awtha athh adm khshthrit amiy uwkhshtrhy tumaya adm khshaythiy amiy madiy." "This Phraortes was an impostor. He thus declared, I am Xathrites, of the race of Cyaxares; I am king of Media."* In giving the following translation I have nothing to say in its favour; it was thrown off as I found it, nearly *verbatim,* without any labour or study; but this I must say, it seems a remarkable coincidence that it should give forth just such language as we might naturally expect from a disappointed and unsuccessful conspirator;—" Behold I Yaja† in captivity and misfortune; governing well the province through a long troublous time, I saw not affliction; a babbling, mischievous spirit flew from province to province, inflaming the mind; vainly I administered justice and mercy, desiring tranquillity and rest; malice grew triumphant

---

* Sir H. Rawlinson says "that the language of Herodotus is in full agreement with that of the Behustan inscriptions." I think this should be reversed, viz., "the language of Rawlinson is *in full agreement with Herodotus.*"

† The Persian word, "Yaja," is synonymous with "fool." "I am Yaja,"—*i.e., I am a fool.*

(literally, *fat.*) Lo! mercy I never expect—our land in trouble, our water in affliction, (and) I in odour and tranquillity like a stagnant pool. I am Yaja. The spirit of the king and his race is sorrow, trouble, the essence of misfortune. To increase in prosperity is vanity; (I) desire life; forgiveness is not to be expected; no mercy will ever be shown to us; our land in trouble, forgiveness in vain, and I in fetters, it is folly to expect mercy; *the die is cast.* I am Yaja! Lo! forgiveness will never be. I am Yaja."

Such is the result of the experimental test of Rawlinson's first ten groups of Persian cuneiform, and of seventy-one groups cut on the dress of Rawlinson's Phraortes, by means of the primitive alphabet. Concluding this part of the subject, with respect to the Behustan alphabet, I may ask for an answer to be given to the following queries:—1st. What occasion is there for two g's, three k's, two h's, and two r's in his alphabet? 2ndly. In his translation, why supply Dh for D, and Mu for M; and in the forty-first letter, why use k for kh? 3rdly. Why supply five letters in the ninth word; and lastly, why is he not content with his own alphabet? Why use one of Lassen's letters in two instances in this short inscription? Rawlinson says he follows the text of 1839. I ask, whose text? His own is dated 1844. If he means Lassen's, that text from 1839 to 1844 differs very materially, as widely as A and Q, J and Z, and SH and R. (*Vide* Rawlinson's Alphabet.) How very necessary it is he should recollect every step taken in this important inquiry?

But let us return and look a little further into Rawlinson's translation of the Black Marble Obelisk, commenced in the preceding chapter. As I have said before, he attempts the translation by means of his self-acknowledged *imperfect Behustan key* of forty letters, which we have just spoken of. Any one at all acquainted with the various cuneiform inscriptions from Persepolis, Behustan, Nakshi-Rustam, Nineveh, and Babylon, must have observed that there is a marked difference in the combination of the various groups of elements or wedges, and that the system of Rawlinson, in making an individual group of such elements in the Persian language a letter, cannot hold good with similar groups of Nineveh or Babylonia, which belonged to a much earlier age and nation. To illustrate this: we know that the English, French, and Latin languages are composed of the same elemental signs or letters, but to produce a word of the same meaning they enter into different combinations. For instance, if I take a group of elemental characters, or one word in English, Dog; another group or word of the same meaning in French, Chien; and another in Latin, Canis; these would be all different combinations, yet precisely one meaning. But if I adopt the Rawlinsonian *imperfect system*, and apply the English group, Dog, to a corresponding group in French, the nearest approach to it would be Doge, with the addition of what I imagine Rawlinson would call a *non-essential*. Now, would it be right to say that it had the same meaning, viz., that a Doge is a Dog, because the groups are similar in form? Again, if I apply the same group, Dog, to the Latin language, the nearest combination to it would be Dogma, with two non-essentials. Again, if I apply the French group Chien to the Latin I should have Chia—"a fig of delicious quality." Would it be proper to say the two words meant the same thing? Yet the Assyrian philologists are still farther a-field in their variants of the same letter. They have formed alphabets differing greatly in number. One has forty, another eighty, another ninety. Then Rawlinson's Assyrian alphabet is composed of one hundred and fifty letters, with five hundred variants, and of which they can give no certain account as to the phonetic power of each letter. Neither does Rawlinson think it of any consequence. They apply this imaginary alphabet to a language that had existed between two and three thousand years earlier, and which has scarcely any or but few corresponding groups to their alphabet. Is it any wonder they are full of doubt, uncertainty, and error? If we compare the Persian groups which form Rawlinson's alphabet with the groups on the Black Marble Obelisk, we shall find only *seven groups* or letters that will at all correspond, viz., k, kh, q, t, f, b and ii; and if we take the various groups of which the Rawlinsonian alphabet is formed, and test them by the primitive, we shall find that each individual Rawlinsonian letter has either a Persian, Arabic, or Hebrew meaning attached to each separate group, as has been noticed before; proving, as I think, beyond doubt that one alphabet was common all over the East, as in modern days—one alphabet for English, French, Spanish, Latin, &c., &c. But to proceed with the Black Marble Obelisk: Rawlinson says that the inscription on it opens with an invocation to the Assyrian gods, and here he makes *the remarkable confession*, "I cannot follow the sense, but *I think* I perceive the following names!" Then follows a list of names taken from the Assyrian mythology, which he subsequently candidly tells us are "*very doubtful, indeed.*" But *why* cannot he follow the sense? He has given us twenty-six lines of cuneiatic groups forming this invocation, all in clear, well-defined characters (of which I can make intelligible sense,) and subsequently he gives us page after page of letter-press—descriptive of battles and sieges, and prisoners taken; of thousands upon thousands slain; cities pillaged and burnt, &c., &c., and yet he cannot follow the sense of the opening invocation! The fact is, there are some very peculiar and complicated groups in the first twenty-six lines which he cannot find in any other inscription (and which I find to be names of individuals,) showing the probability of their being distinctive appellatives of certain individuals who, having distinguished themselves during the reign of the Obelisk king, passed away, and we hear of them no more; just as in modern days we do not find the names of Marlborough, Walpole, or Pitt in the annals of William the Fourth. One of those names is the conjectural distinctive epithet already noticed (Auszits,) and many others, as "Bitzaallini, Achligrou, Ligirr, and Gillirri the supreme king;" if Rawlinson cannot make sense of those groups, of what use I ask, is his alphabet of 150 letters and 500 variants? He then goes on to detail the annals of his ideographical Temen Bar, year by year. I pass over many minor errors until I come to the tenth year, the transactions of which are represented by two lines of groups, containing, according to his system, fifty-four letters. Now, the names of Darius and Sargon are composed of seven groups each, and if we allow four groups to be the average of a word, we shall have not quite fourteen words to record the events of the tenth year, which would give but a very brief account of the year's transactions,—too short, indeed, for Sir H. Rawlinson, for he has given us *twelve lines of letter-press* for the year's annals, containing 120 words! Can there be any truth, I ask again, in such translations? Again, the eleventh year has two and a-half lines of cuneiatic writing, containing eighty-two letters or about twenty words; not very prolific in events, but Sir Henry makes up for it by giving us seventeen and a-half ($17\frac{1}{2}$) lines of letter-press, containing at least 175 words! Where does it all come from? And then again, in contrast with the two last mentioned cases; in the annals of the twenty-fifth year there are sixteen (16) lines of cuneiatic character, and to describe them, we have only seven and a-half ($7\frac{1}{2}$) lines of letter-press. This, of course, is more in accordance with his own system; but if two and a-half ($2\frac{1}{2}$) lines of characters cannot be described with less than one hundred and seventy-five (175) words, it follows that we must have upwards of eleven hundred (1100) words for the sixteen (16) lines, instead of the seventy-five (75) which he has given us. Once more, he says, that " the name of Euphrates is written," and then he gives us five different groups of characters, quite opposite to each other in form, *each one* representing the word " Euphrates," but in *no one instance* out of nine is either of the five groups to be found in the place he has assigned for them. In the twenty-first year he has " the twentieth (20) time I crossed the Euphrates," but the numeral on the obelisk is twenty-one (21,) and in the twenty-fourth year he says, " I crossed the river *Zab*," and he has given us precisely the same groups for *Zab*, as he has all through for Euphrates, What answer can be given to these glaring inconsistencies? I will give the reply in his own words:—" I do not affect to consider my reading of the Obelisk inscription in the light of a critical translation, whenever indeed I have met with a passage of any particular obscurity *I have omitted it :*" (this accounts for his omitting the invocation) " and the interpretation even which I have given of many of the standard expressions *is almost conjectural.*" The following words will show the confidence with which he views his own translation of the events contained in the inscription on the Black Marble Obelisk. He says:—" Of this register (of events) I will now, accordingly, undertake to give an explanation, merely premising that although considerable difficulty still attaches to the pronunciation of the proper names, and although the meaning of particular passages is *still unknown to me,* I hold the accurate ascertainment of the general purport of the legend to be no more subject to controversy than my decipherment of the Persian Behustan inscriptions." Very possible! but still they are very doubtful. Then follow his conjectures respecting the epigraphs,— which I regret I cannot follow, not having a knowledge of his alphabet or of the variants; but this I know that in the fourth epigraph where he states that the tribute is that of " Sut-pal-adan," there is not any group (that he has previously stated) to stand for " Sut" in the whole epigraph; there are many " Pal's," (*Vide* Plate IV., fig. 1) but not one " Adan " in the epigraph ; of course the variants will be brought in to supply their place. But what can be said of such a system, where the interpreters can pick and choose from a lot of 500, and just make what they please?

Again, speaking of the various articles which compose the five tributary offerings, he says:—" Gold, silver, pearls and gems, ebony and ivory, may be made out with more or less accuracy, but I *cannot conjecture* (wonderful!) the nature of many of the offerings; camels I find under the designation of ' *beasts of the desert with the double back.'* " Why, according to his own system this designation would occupy as much space as is assigned for the whole epigraph, leaving no room for Forster's " honeycomb tripe, or paunches uncut;" or for the elephant, monkeys, and other animals, which are to be seen with the camels. Is it at all probable or reasonable to suppose that the ancients, who were obliged to record the annals of their kings and their literature upon stones, would adopt such a round about way of naming an animal when one word would suffice? And that one word (according to the primitive alphabet) we have in each epigraph under where the camels are found, and no more—בכן (BKN,) the נ (N) commuted for ר (R,) which is quite legitimate—בכר (BKR,) "young camels." Then, again, we have the word AKKG, which is under the "capræ œgag-rus," or Assyrian goat, which appears to be a favourite oblation to their gods, and as such an acceptable offering or tribute, the exact figure is seen on Face B, behind the rhinoceros. And, lastly, there are several figures bearing bundles of wood (it must be precious wood to be brought as tribute to a king,) and here we have the name of the most costly wood that was known in the East, אאלמז (AALMZ,) the ז (Z) commuted for ג (G) to suit modern orthography—THE ALMUG. The word is seen in the left-hand corner of the fourth group of figures (Face D,) and this *almug-wood* was used for ornamentation in palaces, and for musical instruments.

CHAPTER IX.

Cylinder of Tiglath Pilezer—Fox Talbot's defence of Sir H. Rawlinson—Author's answer to it—Great inconsistencies in the translation, &c., &c.—Rawlinson's confidence in his own works—Rawlinson's anachronism requiring explanation—Author's translation of the three gradines of the Black Marble Obelisk—Author's translation from the winged figure—Conclusion.

LET us now look a little into the celebrated translation from the supposed cylinder of Tiglath Pilezer. In support of the theory of Sir H. Rawlinson Mr. Fox Talbot says:—" For several years, and almost from the first discovery of the Assyrian inscriptions two rival scholars have been separately engaged in the work of interpretation, and some of the chief discoveries are due to their sagacity, and each of them far from acquiescing indolently in the other's opinion, has always shown a disposition to criticise, and examine them narrowly; the result of their long and careful examination has, however, been a substantial agreement as to the nature, sense, and meaning of the inscriptions, the pronunciation of the words, and the almost complete revivification as it were of a long and totally forgotten language: an individual scholar might, perhaps, be led by his fancy in such an inquiry; but it is quite impossible that two intelligent men inquiring independently should agree respecting the syllabic value of one or two hundred crabbed and complicated symbols, and a vast number of words formed out of such syllables, and also as to the true intent and meaning of long historic statements in those phrases of a nearly unknown language, if there were no real basis of truth on which they had each separately reared their edifice."

In answer to these statements I contend that there is nothing extraordinary in the apparent agreement of the Assyrian philologists (even supposing they *were* all agreed, which is far from being the case), when we know that they work with the same alphabet, but differ in some of their letters as they lean to some of the earlier systems of Grotefend, Burnouf, and Lassen. Let us suppose a case:—A slab is found with an ancient Greek inscription on it. A copy of the inscription is sent to a professor of languages in each of the English universities for translation. Should we be surprised, or think it anything remarkable, if there happened to be a general agreement in the translations, when all translated by means of the same alphabet? There *might* be some trifling variations, but they would certainly agree in the main. But not so with this cylinder of Tiglath Pilezer. It is true that Messrs. Rawlinson, Talbot, and Oppert agree in the names of thirty-nine countries, or nearly so, "with one or two doubtful exceptions; *at the same time, however, it is to be remarked that this agreement is no doubt to be attributed to their having adopted the values proposed previously by Rawlinson and Hinckes.*" And here the agreement ends. Out of fifty-four paragraphs there are more than thirty that do *not* agree, and there are many extraordinary variations, a few of which I shall enumerate. Thus, in the fourth paragraph, Rawlinson says:—"Having committed to my hand their *valiant and warlike servants.*" Of the same groups of characters, Talbot makes, "I have grasped in battle their *mighty weapons in my hand.*" And the same group Dr. Oppert renders, "They spoke to me their language (that is,) extensive domination of *the fore part of my ships!*" Is not this last quite unintelligible? Where is the agreement? Again, in the fifth paragraph, according to Rawlinson, we have, "their *moveables*, their wealth, and their valuables I plundered, to a countless amount." The same sentence, rendered by Talbot, is, "their *women*, and their . . . and their . . . . abundantly I carried off." Once more, in the thirty-sixth paragraph, Rawlinson has, "Under the auspices of my guardian deity *Hercules*, two soss of *lions* fell before me and 800 LIONS, in my chariots, in my exploratory journeys I laid low." (Why does he say "*two soss?*" Why cannot he keep to the text and say 120.) Of the same passage Mr. Fox Talbot makes, "In the *Ninev* my guardian deity, 120 *buffaloes* in the conflict of the chase on my lands, I slew, and 800 *of them* in my chariots, in enclosed parks I destroyed." In another place Rawlinson has "wild buffaloes," and Dr. Hinckes "wild elephants." Nimroud the mighty hunter must sink into utter insignificance, after such a royal sportsman! Can it be possible that three gentlemen of such acknowledged learning can really believe in their own system, when such palpable contradictions are to be found in their various translations of the same passage? Nor is this all; they cannot even agree in the names of the gods. Thus, Rawlinson has, in one instance, "The gods Hercules and Nergal," and Talbot has "The gods Niniv and Sidu." They agree in the name of the great Anu, the first of the sacred Triad, but they all disagree in the second, for Rawlinson has "Vul;" Talbot, "Yem;" Hinckes, "Iv;" and Oppert, "Ao." And lastly, with respect to names, we have in the forty-fourth paragraph the following varying interpretations:—

Rawlinson: "The beloved child of *Bazanpalakura*."
Talbot: "The *fourth* descendant of *Ninivbalushat*."
Oppert: "The *fifth* descendant of *Ninip-pal-ukin*."*

These are only a few out of a multitude of examples that could be cited, showing indisputably that their agreement in any case is purely conjectural. The two principal philologists, moreover, are at direct variance in the most essential points, the chronological and historical: for both Sir H. Rawlinson and Dr. Hinckes state that the principal events recorded upon the above-mentioned cylinder took place 1120 B.C., and yet there is no mention in Biblical history, or in Josephus, of any Assyrian king invading the

---

* Extract from a letter by Mrs. Caroline Frances Cornwallis to Samuel Birch, Esq.:—"Can we depend on Major Rawlinson's Readings of the Cuneiform Inscriptions? My faith is not very firm in his interpretations, but perhaps your treaty with the Egyptian king may give a little more certainty to his *conjectures*. Not having Mr. ——'s plenary inspiration, I am troubled with a certain feeling that I know nothing about the matter, but that when names are expressed, it is possible that they *may be imagined rather than deciphered*."—*Correspondence of C. F. Cornwallis.* London: 1864. *(Just Published.)*

country of Judea at the time specified in their translation. The Bible is very clear upon this point (2 Kings, xv., 27, 29.) "In the two and fiftieth year of Azariah, king of Judah, Pekah the son of Remaliah began to reign over Israel in Samaria, (and reigned) twenty years;" and twenty-ninth verse, "In the days of Pekah, king of Israel, came Tiglath Pilezer, king of Assyria, and took Ijon, and Abel Beth Maachah, and Janoah, and Kedesh, and Hazor, and Gilead, and Galilee, all the land of Naphthali, and carried them captive to Assyria." And this is strongly corroborated by Josephus (Book IX., chap. xi., sec. 1.): "Now; this Pekah held the government twenty years, and proved a wicked man and a transgressor. But the king of Assyria, whose name was Tiglath Pilezer, when he had made an expedition against the Israelites, and had overrun all the land of Gilead, and the region beyond Jordan, and the adjoining country, which is called Galilee, and Kadesh, and Hazor, he made the inhabitants prisoners, and transplanted them into his own kingdom." Not a word is said here about Egypt. These events took place, according to Biblical chronology, 740 B.C., and consequently there is a discrepancy of nearly 400 years. Mr. Fox Talbot reads from the inscription that the invasion of the aforesaid king was into Syria and Egypt:— "All the provinces of Musri (*i.e:*, lower Egypt,) I ravaged, their armies I destroyed, and I burnt their cities." This interpretation is partly supported by Sir H. Rawlinson, who says that Tiglath Pilezer invaded Palestine and conquered all before him, from beyond the Euphrates to the " Upper sea of the setting sun" (the Mediterranean). But Dr. Hinckes, in flat contradiction to this, says, "*I am satisfied*, and I expressed my conviction most decidedly in notes to my translation, that the countries *supposed to be Egypt* lay to the north-east of Korsabad, and that the *supposed expedition* into Syria and the Mediterranean WAS ONE INTO ARMENIA AND THE BLACK SEA." It is evident from what the doctor says here, that he thinks Rawlinson's and Talbot's translations are mostly imaginary or conjectural. Now, after viewing all those glaring discrepancies and contradictions, who will be bold enough to say there is any dependence to be placed on the "Literary Inquest,"—or as some call it, "The final ordeal,"—when the three most celebrated of Assyrian philologists are thus found to be in direct antagonism to each other?

It is much to be wished that these three eminent scholars should give us a plain explanation of the *means* by which they have arrived at the phonetic power of each particular letter or syllable, so that their readers might be put in a position to judge for themselves. But what, in point of fact, does Sir H. Rawlinson say upon this point. He says:—"*I am neither able, nor is it of any consequence*, after the lapse of so many years, to *describe the means* by which I ascertained the power of each particular letter, or to determine the respective dates of the discoveries." Now, this, to say the least of it, is a very off-hand and unsatisfactory method of getting over difficulties. Does Sir H. Rawlinson imagine that we are to take all that he chooses to put into print, without examination or question? "There are two considerations which seem to justify us in expecting some more minute information on this head. The first is *the confidence* which the discoverers evidently repose in their conclusions; which is such that one of them (Dr. Hincks) has not only presented us with the first of a series of Assyrian Grammar, but has even ventured to employ *his assumed* knowledge of that language to the criticism of other cognate dialects, which have been known and studied ever since they have ceased to be spoken. The second is that—without venturing for a moment to question the profound learning and acute sagacity of the discoverers—the more tentative the process, the more conjectural the result, and the smaller the number of witnesses (at present not much above the Mosaic minimum) by which the soundness of that result is attested, or who are competent to give evidence in regard to it, the more ample we naturally desire their testimony to be that we may be put as much as possible in a position to form an opinion for ourselves."

But as a strong proof of the confidence Sir Henry Rawlinson had in his own works, let us take what he published in the year 1847, in the *Royal Asiatic Journal* (Vol. X., page 13.) Speaking of the Behustan inscription, he there says:—" In the present case, then, I do put forth a claim to originality, as having put forth to the world a literal and, as I believe, a correct grammatical translation of nearly two hundred lines of cuneiform writing (since augmented to four hundred,) a memorial of Darius Hystaspes, the greater part of which is in so perfect a state as to afford ample and certain grounds for a minute orthographical and etymological analysis; and the purport of which to the historian must, I think, be of fully equal interest with the peculiarities of its language to the philologist." Again, in the sixteenth page of the same volume, he says:—" In February of the present year (1846 or 1847,) I took the precaution of forwarding to the Royal Asiatic Society a literal translation of *every portion* of the Persian writing at Behustan, and of thus placing beyond the power of dispute the claim of the society at date (February, 1846 or 1847) to the results which are published in the following memoir." Now let it be remarked that the foregoing extract was written several years previous to the discovery of the Black Marble Obelisk by Layard. Yet we find in the year 1850 or 1851 Sir Henry speaking in this style:—" Many of the standard expressions at Behustan—such as "*The rebels having assembled their forces, came against me offering battle, I fought with them and defeated them*'—PROVE TO HAVE BEEN ADOPTED VERBATIM FROM THE ASSYRIAN ANNALS." This requires a pause! Does Sir H. Rawlinson mean to say that Darius Hystaspes copied from the Assyrian inscriptions? If so, what authority has he for the assertion? since it is certain that Nineveh's palaces had been destroyed many years before the birth of Darius, and it was only in the palaces of Nineveh that any records were found. Sir H. Rawlinson goes on to say:—" It was indeed the discovery of known passages of this sort *in the Obelisk inscription* that first gave me an insight into the general purport of the legend" (*i.e.*, the Behustan inscription.) But how is this to be reconciled with the former part of his statement, when the Obelisk was not known to exist for several years subsequent to the completion of the Behustan legend? Sir Henry *had finished* the Persian inscription in the early part of the year 1846 or 1847; but he did not see the Obelisk until his arrival in London, in the middle of the year 1849! This is an inconsistency which requires explanation.*

In pointing out these obvious discrepancies, my sole design is to exhibit the results of a system which I firmly believe will ultimately prove to be wholly erroneous. The subject I consider to be one of great and vital importance, and as I claim to be the discoverer of a new system, I am compelled, in proving the truth of my own theory, also to show the errors and inconsistencies of previous systems. At the same time, while I firmly believe that my system is founded upon truth and reason, I think that it is subject to many modifications, and that it can only be brought to perfection by gentlemen of profound abilities as Oriental scholars, and then I hope that the great problem of the primitive language will be solved. Having said this much, parenthetically, I shall proceed to show that it is next to an impossibility for me to give anything like a correct translation of any of the inscriptions, for several reasons. First, I am 16,000 miles distance from the originals, and have only printed copies to refer to. Secondly, those copies are so full of errors that I think it labour in vain to attempt any more: errors which Messrs. Rawlinson, Hinckes, and

* Monsieur De Saulcy, a member of the French Institute, a man of science, an extensive traveller in the East, and a *real* discoverer himself in epigraphy. This antiquary convicts the readings of Rawlinson, which reveal to us the lost names of certain kings of the Assyrian dynasties, of being *left destitute of proof*, of being *improbable in themselves*, or at *variance with each other*. He substantiates this triple charge against Rawlinson's Pantheon, taking the principal divinities, personage by personage, to the number of over a score; in conclusion, however, he says, with sarcastic deference, that he "*denies nothing*, but merely waits until Rawlinson gives *some proofs of his revelations;* and this, incumbent even in religion, is indispensable in all science, and was imperative in the present subject, where the discoverer *pretends alone* to have the key to the exploration of the cuneiform writings." It is also the advice I would convey to your British readers, who, indeed, appear themselves to have tacitly taken a similar course, if one may judge from the little noise they make about so startling a publication.—*Athenæum Francais*. And to say the truth, the publication seems *to merit the severest treatment*, adds the editor of the *Journal of Sacred Literature*.

I

Layard would only call *non-essentials*, such as the omission of elements or wedges from some groups, the substitution of one group for another, and the alteration of the figure of an element. For instance, the Awleph (or A) I find in some cases is drawn out, or elongated, and consequently it becomes the Lamed (or L;) and, *vice versâ*, the Lamed gets shortened and becomes A. Sometimes Tsade (or TS) gets placed upright and has the appearance of CH; and again, the Zain will assume the perpendicular and become the Beth. Now, all these changes are looked upon as *non-essentials*, and may be tolerated on the imperfect Behustan system; but with the primitive system, where every element is a letter, it would greatly, if not fatally interfere with the truth of the translation. Therefore, although it was at first my intention to make a translation of the whole of the inscription on the Black Marble Obelisk, I shall be obliged to defer it for the present. I have made an attempt of the first three gradines, subject to the above disadvantages. I will not say anything in its favour, only this much, that I can *follow the sense*, and I *do not think I can perceive* any of the names of the Assyrian mythology. It begins with a proclamation from the supreme king, Gillirri,* appointing one Tsaallni to be governor over the conquered people of *Lailirou*,† and stating that their king will be cared for:—" Gillirri entered the city and took captive the king; but fearful and mystic cries found favour or pleased the feeble monarch. Gillirri appoints the friend of

---

* In the third volume of the *Journal of Sacred Literature*, page 476, there is a paper by Mr. W. H. Ormsby, wherein the writer states that, " Gimirad, or chief bowman or chief of the Gimir, had settled in Shinar and founded a Scythic kingdom." May not this be the same individual as the one mentioned above ? We know that the liquids L and M interchange one with the other; therefore *Gillirri* might have become Gimmirri or Gimir, or *vice versâ*.

† Can this be the name mentioned in Genesis xvi. 14, with a slight alteration in the orthography ? It is well known that people in ancient as well as in modern days congregate and take up their dwelling-place near a spring or well of water (as is proved in Genesis xxv. 11, " And Isaac dwelt by the well LAHAIROI, ") and possibly became the founder of a township or city afterwards called LAILIROU.

Tsaallni, chief who will not fail by firmness of mind to collect the tribute. Second gradine:—"And make it known that through the intercession of Tsaallni I will not fail to save some approved and selected Llen, Auszits, and the chief; and thou Tsaallni preserve from trouble Lalagees,* who brought in the tribute. Auszits fought fearfully to prevent the entering of Aram. I will confine him securely with Blaal, Ligirr, and Ahhligron their chief, whom if the people had assisted him (no) trouble would have entered *Lailirou*. Proclaim! Nothing shall distress the land during the sojourn of the king, Gillirri the triumphant!" Third gradine:— "(Obliteration, Proclamation to the town) and the city! And I, the supreme king, will imprison all rebellious to my authority, and compel them to accept the new governor. Assuredly the towns (obliteration, will submit as well as) the city. Be it known unto all that the chief governor of the people of Lailirou will rebuild the walls or fortifications, and lo! they will behold them (obliteration, like as a) friend seen in the time of trouble. The chief Tsaallni will compel the governor by the fourteenth day of the month Zou to abide (his word,) &c. &c." Thus it will be seen that whatever I attempt I can elicit sense, and in this last case a continuous narrative. What remains it is impossible for me to say at present; but I shall be most anxious to resume my studies when I know I can do so with certainty. There is another subject alluded to in page 73, which I must say something about, viz., a slab with a representation of a winged figure, or Assyrian priest, bearing on his left arm a kid of the *capra œgagrus* (a goat inhabiting the European Alps as well as the Asiatic ranges.) and, it will be observed, an animal of the same species as is seen on the Black Marble Obelisk. The figure bears something in his right hand not clearly defined, but having some resemblance to

* Has this name any connection with the Leleges we read of in ancient history, a collection of people of different nations, derived from λεγω, "to gather," as its name imports, so named from Lelex, an Egyptian who came with a colony to Megara, where he reigned 200 years before the Trojan war, about A.M. 2650, or about the time of Joshua?

a large ear of corn; he wearing a robe reaching down to the heels, beautifully embroidered and fringed, with large tassels hanging from the waist, and a similar under-dress reaching to the knees, and with bracelets on the wrists with rosette clasps. The inscription of sixteen lines are cut or engraved across the lower part of the dress, through the interstices and sinuosities of the fringe, which made some portions of the inscription very difficult to copy. The inscription begins with the usual formula:—" Proclamation! Palace, together with Aashoik, the wrath of God abideth in and around, and will destroy them; but I will dwell among my kindred. O that thou wouldst cry aloud and scatter (or break to pieces) the multitude of stone gods, and show me the extreme beauty of the true God, and the manifestations of his glory. Hasten my desires. Light! shine (forth) and spread around the eternal and unchangeable Supreme." Second line:—"And thine altar shall be covered with that which covereth the top* (with the glory of Him who is above all.) O that thou wouldst attend to my prayer, if thy wrath covereth with confusion, if thou art He that dwelt, and that spread around that which covereth the top (goodness, and mercy, and truth,) many of thy desolate ones will be swiftly taken away (by him) who covereth the top. Repent! the wrath of Him, the eternal, cometh quickly, and will assuredly curse and destroy the rock, my god."

This is the substance of two lines only, and the legend applicable to the device; and so it is in every instance, on the application of the nineteen letters of the primitive alphabet, without monograms, ideographs, or variants. Those inconsistencies and contradictions

---

* Does not this appear to be an allusion to the altar and mercy-seat of the Israelites, taken by the Assyrians, in all probability at the sacking of Samaria, and preserved, perhaps, in the palace of which this slab formed a part:—" And the cherubim shall stretch forth their wings on *high, covering the mercy-seat* with their wings." "And thou shalt put the mercy-seat *above* upon the ark, and there I will meet with thee, from above the mercy-seat, from between the two cherubim." Or has it rather reference to a remarkable imitation of the Divine presence mentioned by Philostratus, and noticed (page 60.)

CONCLUSION. 117

which I have pointed out, might be multiplied *ad infinitum*, but I think I have said enough to convince the candid reader that the systems hitherto propounded cannot be true, and I may add, without egotism, that the theory submitted in the present work is at once simple, practicable, and carries on it the face of truth. Let not the great philologists throw it aside as unworthy of notice, or with the feeling that no good can come out of Nazareth. Let them rather condescend to test this new theory with the same zeal as they have shown with their self-acknowledged imperfect key, and possibly they may find that the conjectures of many scholars will turn out to be true,—" That the earliest of the three orders of cuneiform character imprisons *a captive and dumb Semitic speech;*" and may also be able to answer an important question put by an eminent writer: " Where may lie the tomb of the mother of the Semitic family, so soft and artless in her expressions, so unsophisticated in her ways, who utters no word but burns with life, who is too earnest to smile, too impassioned to argue, too confiding to reason, whose passions seem exhaustless, and her intellect scarcely appreciable, the woman, *par excellence*, of human languages? Like the grave of her greatest prophet, it lies concealed from human eyes by the marge of some brook, on some Armenian hill, by some Mesopotamian watercourse. All that we know leads us to believe in *one primitive Semitic speech.*"

This fact has, in our opinion, been brought full into the light of day by the indefatigable researches of Layard, but still awaits the magic wand of the true philologist to bring it into life. The modern interpreters have been trying their various systems now for more than sixty years, and they are as far off from any certain and definite result as when they began. It is surely high time they essayed a trial of some other system.

I have noticed in a former part of this work that I discovered the numerals while forming a lexicon for facilitating the translating the whole of the inscription on the Black Marble Obelisk. I had completed the sixtieth word of the letter A when the numerals put a stop for a time to my lexicon-making; and the subsequent discovery that through the inaccuracy of the authorised copy I could not depend upon any word, has caused me to give it up until a more favourable opportunity. In Plate III. the reader will see nine simple words from the lexicon, letter A, and the method of reading the more complicated groups in the adjoining column. This diagram (Plate III.) shows the *truth-speaking simplicity of the system.*

What is the conclusion, then, that we must perforce come to? All ages and all nations, ancient and modern, point to the east, of which Nineveh formed the centre, and from which radiated to north, south, east, and west all the knowledge of the arts, sciences, and literature which have made man "a little lower than the angels, and crowned him with glory and honour." Can there be a doubt that Nineveh was the recipient of the primitive alphabet and the art of writing from the patriarch Shem, who, in his turn, received it from his father, Noah, and whose grandfather, Lamech, lived many years contemporaneously with Adam, *who received it directly from God?* In this age of marvellous discoveries what may we expect if men of such profound learning as Sir H. Rawlinson, Dr. Hinckes, and Mr. Fox Talbot, concentrating their abilities upon this interesting subject, and with the aid of this new alphabet, may not bring out of those ancient inscriptions? Who can tell what new and important historical truths may be brought to light respecting the early history of the world, in corroboration and full elucidation of the inspired narrative in the Old Testament?

In conclusion, I hope that the subject matter of the present treatise will be apology sufficient for any errors that may be found in it. Nothing could have induced the author to have written this work but a deep conviction of the truth of the system he propounds, and from an almost overwhelming sense of its great importance. It has been carried on through difficulties almost unparalleled; but faith in the truth of his theory, and hope in its final results, has cheered him on to its completion.

FINIS.

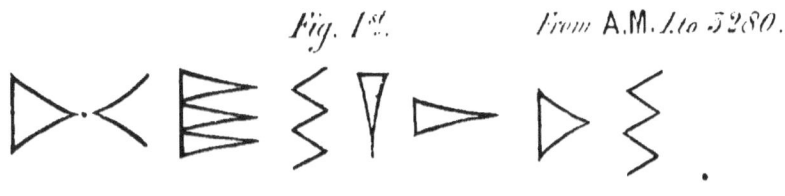

Fig. 1st. From A.M. 1 to 3280.

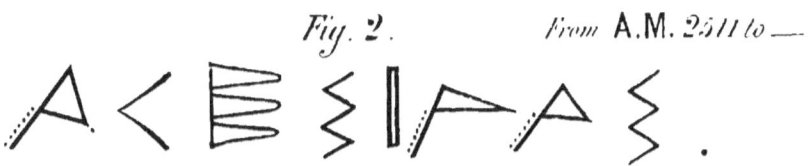

Fig. 2. From A.M. 2511 to ___

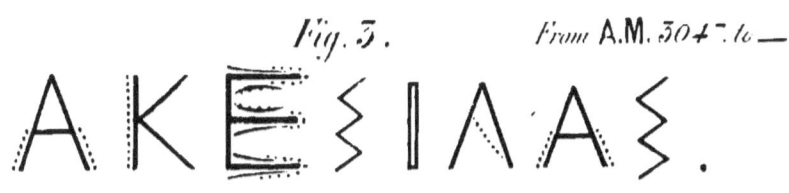

Fig. 3. From A.M. 3047 to ___

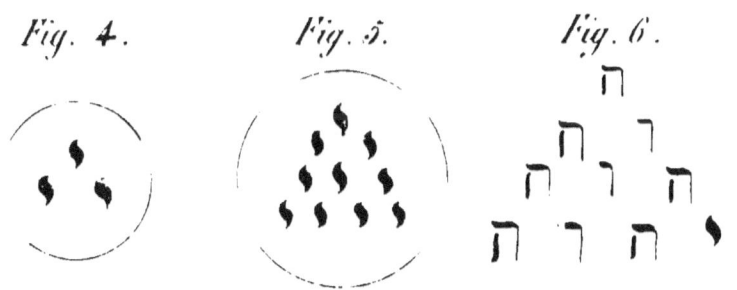

Fig. 4.   Fig. 5.   Fig. 6.

Plate 2nd. Revd C. Forster's Alphabet.

			Primitive System
1	⋈ or Y	The Greek or Hamyaritic B or D.	A G "to bind"
2	⋈̄	Hamyaritic & Ethiopic H	LN "to dwell or abide".
3	▽⊲	Greek K	ug or ig "pained"
4	⊲	Greek V or N	G
5	⊵▽	Greek E	CHU, "Show, declare, or Proclaim."
6	▷ or ⊳▽	Greek P or Hamyaritic	AI, "Country" or Bou "to go in or out" or "to reign".
7	⋈̄†	Ethiopic †	Lou, "O! that thou wouldst."
Figure 1st. ✱ ✱ ▽ ▷	ر) or ر) ك Hamyaritic B or D	Dal, or dabab.	Fig. 2. ▷⋈ ⋈▷ ▷▽ ✱ ✱ ⋈ Over a castle taken by storm "Those dwelling in filth and laden with crimes I scattered with the stone." ▷⋈ ⋈ ▽ ⊳

Plate 2nd A.

Groups	Arabic	Mr Forster's Translation
1. ▽𒀭△	دس dus	A Paunch, or Honey comb, &c. &c.
2. ▽𒀭△	دسدس dusdus	Dentes deflui, or shed teeth.
3. ▽𒀭△	دسو dusu	Mila genus. Grain.
4. ▽𒀭△	دس dus	quod frequenter pendition tributum or frequently paid tribute.
5. △𒀭△▽▽▽		Also shed teeth.

Author's Translation.

| 6. ▽𒀭△ | ⁓⁓⁓ | "Precious treasure stored up." |

The four concluding words of each Epigraph.

| 7. ▽𒀭△ ▽𒀭△ ▽▽▽ | | "The Precious Treasure to be stored safely by order of the Lochu, i.e. a River or Governor of a Town, or District. |

Plate 3.

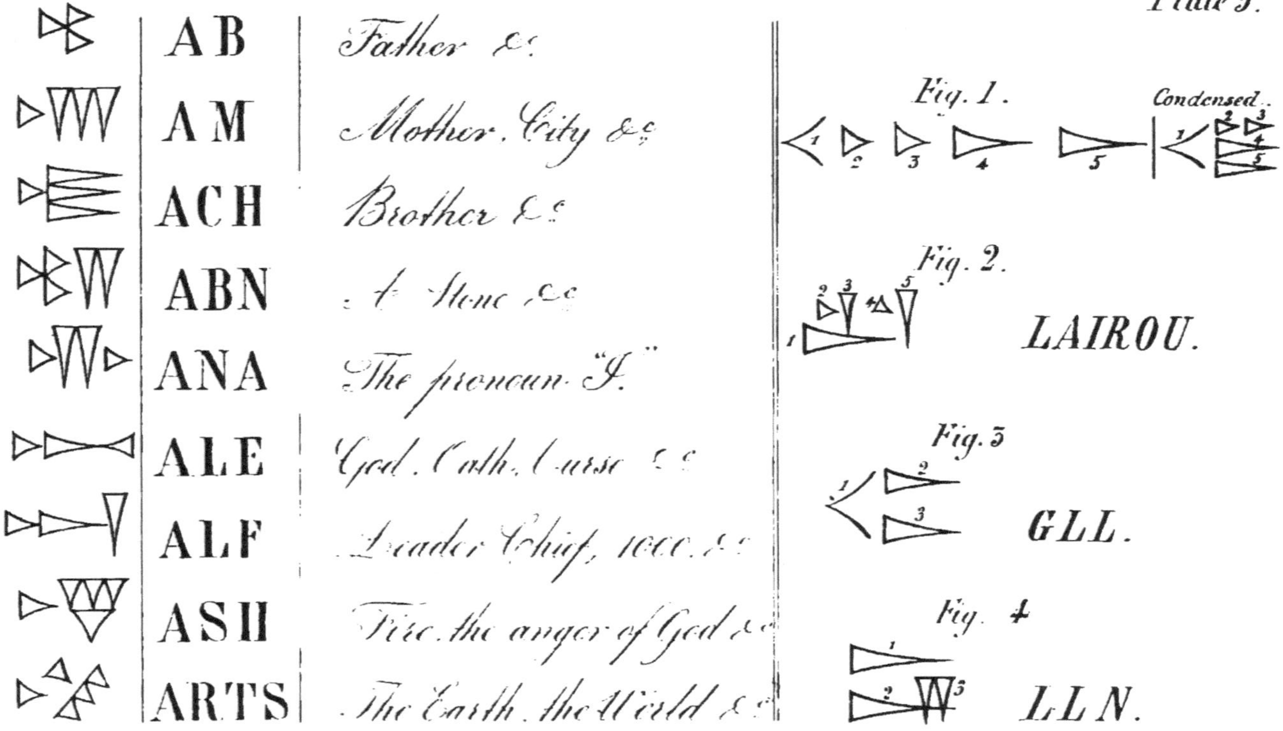

Fig. 1.   Condensed.

LAIROU.

Fig. 2.

Fig. 3.   GLL.

Fig. 4.   LLN.

AB	Father &c.	
AM	Mother, City &c.	
ACH	Brother &c.	
ABN	A Stone &c.	
ANA	The pronoun "I."	
ALE	God, Oath, Curse &c.	
ALF	Leader, Chief, 1000 &c.	
ASH	Fire, the anger of God &c.	
ARTS	The Earth, the World &c.	

Plate 4.

Fig. 1st 
▽▽ Bar of Pul
Hinckess numeral
7

Fig. 2.

1. רחֻב רֹם אֶֽל חֻמצֹּר
2. BW⊽ ⊽X BW ⊽⊠⊽
3. B∧K∧∥Σ BN K≢R

"They shew will be built esp like a seeh."

Fig. 3.

BW⊽ ⊠ V ⊳⊳⊠ ⊳⊠ ⊽⊽
BM ou CHu ou AASH o IK
    shew "together with."

High place, declare. Australeih.
or Palace.   proclaim.

Plate 5.

Fig. 1   *Fig. 2. (i)*   *Fig. 3.*   *Fig. 4.*   *Fig. 5.*   *Fig. 6.*   *Fig. 7.*

I am   *Darius*

Fig. 8.   *Fig. 9.*   *Fig. 10.*   *Fig. 11.*   *Fig. 12.*   *Fig. 13.*   *Fig. 14.*   *Fig. 15.*   *Fig. 16.*   *Fig. 17.*

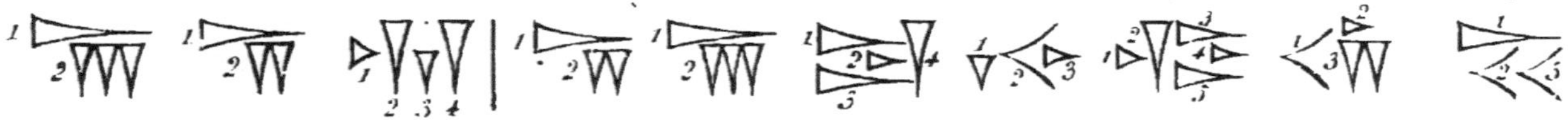

A   D   M   ,   D   A   R   Y   W   I1   sh.

	Phoenician	Palmyrene	Modern Hebrew	Roman
Auf an Ox	ⵄ.⼤	א.א	א	A
Bet House	ⴹ	ⴺ	ב	B
Gi Ca	ⵏ	ⵤ	ג	G
Da Ten	ⴽ.ⵡ	ⵞ	ד	D
	ⴻ	ⴺ.ⴺ	ה	E
Va Hoo	ⵯ.⵰	ⵞ	ו	F or V
Z A	⵮	ⵝ	ז	Z
Ch	ⴲ	ⵝ	ח	CH
I	ⵑ	ⴷ	ִ	I
K	ⵠ	ⵝ	כ	K or Q
La or Ox	ⵍ.⵰	ⵝ	ל	L
M Fe	ⵯ	M	מנ	M
Nun	ⵯ	ⵞ.⵰.ⵑ	נו	N
Sa P	ⵙ	ⵞ	סנ	S
Ain	ⵔ	ⵯ	ע	O
Ts Fish	ⵯ	ⵯ	צנ	TS
Re H	ⵯ.ⵯ	ⵯ	ר	R
Sh To	ⵯ	ⵯ	ש	SH
Ta C	ⵯ.†	ⵯ	ת	T

Published to Illustrate "The Ancient Ones of the Earth."

St Martin. Bernouf. Lassen.

R	B	.....	B	B
a	m	m	m	m
e	i	hm	m	m
?	gh	gh	gh	ah
m	n	n	n	n
....	....	n	n	n
....	....	English n	n	n
e	h	y	y	y
....	r	r	r	r
ch	L	sh	r	R
V	g	V	V	V
i	i	W	W	W
S	G	English		S
ch	ch	sh	.....	sh
e	Z	Z	Z	Z
ou	a	H	h	h

Plate 8

1836.39–44   1836 39–44

#	sign	Grotefend	St.Martin	Burnouf	Lassen		Rawlinson	#	sign	Grotefend	St.Martin	Burnouf	Lassen		Rawlinson
1	𒀸	(;a)	a	a	a	a	a	21			V	R	B	.....	B	B	B
2		ó	y	o	i	i	i	i	22			o	a	m	m	m	m	m
3		u	ou	u	u	u	u	u	23			H	e	i	hm	m	m	m soft
4		é	e	k	k	k	k	k	24			K?	?	gh	gh	gh	ah	ah
5		kh	kh	kh	kh	kh	kh	k	25			tsch	m	n	n	n	n	n
6		Z	h	Q	a	a	a	Q	26			.....	.....	.....	n	n	n	h wn n
7		ü	?	u	gh	g	g	g	27			.....	.....	.....	English	n	n	n
8		Z	.....	gh	gh	gh	gh	gh	28			h	e	k	y	y	y	J J
9		ó	e	v	i	y	k	k	29			R.	.....	r	r	r	r	R.
10		dj	?	gh	g	dj	g	g	30			sch	ch	S	sh	r	R	R
11		ny	?	h	n	n	J	Z	31			g	V	g	V	V	V	V
12		m	t	t	t	t	t	t	32			e	i	i	W	W	W	W
13		th	dh	T	t	t	th	dh	33			S	S	S	English	S	S	S
14		i	h	y	ξ	th	th	θ	34			sch	ch	ch	sh	.....	sh	Sh.
15		m	?	L	k	tch	.....	kh	35			gh.	c	Z	z	Z	Z	Z
16		n	n	th	t	t	tr	thr	36			a	ou	a	H	h	h	H
17		D	D	D	D	D	D	D	37			h	h	.....	.....	y	English	n
18		Z	.....	gh	dh	dh	dh	Dh	38			.....	.....	.....	.....	.....	his	dah
19		Br:P	P	P	P	P	P	P	39			.....	.....	.....	.....	.....	.....	bimi
20		So ph	.....	f	f	f	f	f	40			Sign	of	disjunction	universally	adopted

Plate 9.

Numerals as seen on the Black marble Obelisk.

1						Face B	line 96
2						" "	97
3						" "	99
4	.....					" "	100
5						Layards Monuments of Nineveh 7 line	102
6						Layards M.N. Plate 2. line 9.	104
7						" "	107
8						" C	
9						" "	126
10						" "	132
11						" "	141
12						" " D	146
13						The numeral obliterated	156
14							159
15							174
16		...d above, are as seen in Sir H. Rawlinson's copy.					

Assyrian Numerals, as seen on the Black marble Obelisk.

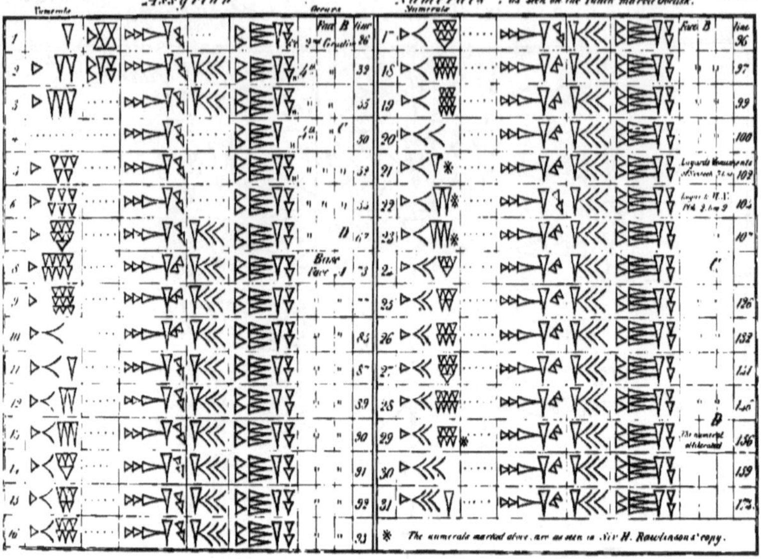

www.ingramcontent.com/pod-product-compliance
Lightning Source LLC
Chambersburg PA
CBHW030252170426
43202CB00009B/711